SPSS® for the Macintosh®: Operations Guide

SPSS Inc.

SPSS Inc.
444 N. Michigan Avenue
Chicago, Illinois 60611
Tel: (312) 329-3500
Fax: (312) 329-3668

SPSS International BV
P.O. Box 115
4200 AC Gorinchem
The Netherlands
Tel: +31.1830.36711
Fax: +31.1830.35839

For more information about SPSS® software products, please write or call

Marketing Department
SPSS Inc.
444 North Michigan Avenue
Chicago, IL 60611
312/329-3500

In Europe and the Middle East, please write or call

SPSS International B.V.
P.O. Box 115
4200 AC Gorinchem
The Netherlands
+31.1830.36711
Twx: 21019 (SPSS nl)
Fax: +31.1830.35839

Preface

SPSS® is a comprehensive, integrated system for statistical data analysis. In SPSS® for the Macintosh®, the SPSS system includes not only the reliable, tested statistical routines for which SPSS software is known, but also a menu-based command generator, context-sensitive help, an online glossary, extensive editing capabilities, and other features designed to help you work efficiently with SPSS.

SPSS for the Macintosh consists of a base system and several add-on options. Available documentation is outlined here and discussed in more detail in "SPSS for the Macintosh Documentation."

Manuals for the Base System.   Documentation for the base system consists of three manuals:

- *SPSS Base System User's Guide* shows how to use SPSS commands to manage and analyze data.
- *SPSS Reference Guide* documents and gives examples of the SPSS commands in the base system and Advanced Statistics option.
- *SPSS for the Macintosh: Operations Guide* (this book) explains how to run SPSS in the Macintosh environment, and indicates the few commands that behave differently in SPSS for the Macintosh from the way they are documented in the user and reference guides.

SPSS Options.   Each of the options for SPSS for the Macintosh comes with a corresponding manual:

- *SPSS Advanced Statistics User's Guide* contains discussions of advanced statistical analyses.
- *SPSS Trends* documents SPSS's complete time series analysis and forecasting tool.
- *SPSS Tables* documents the SPSS TABLES procedure, which presents data in presentation quality tables.
- *SPSS Categories* documents SPSS's conjoint and optimal scaling procedures.

Compatibility. SPSS Inc. warrants that SPSS for the Macintosh and enhancements are designed for personal computers in the Macintosh Plus, Macintosh SE and Macintosh II lines with a hard disk and at least 2MB RAM. 4MB or more is preferred, and is required in order to use MultiFinder. Version 6 or higher of the Apple System Software should be used. A math coprocessor is strongly recommended.

Serial Numbers. Your serial number is your identification number with SPSS Inc. You will need this serial number when you call SPSS Inc. for information regarding support, payment, a defective diskette, or an upgraded system.

The serial number can be found on the first program diskette in your system, labeled B1. Before using the system, please copy this number to the **registration card.**

Registration Card. STOP! Before continuing on, *fill out and send us your registration card.* Until we receive your registration card, you have an unregistered system. Even if you have previously sent a card to us, please fill out and return the card enclosed in your SPSS for the Macintosh package.

Note: if your current order includes add-on options in addition to the base system, you can return a single card.

Registering your system entitles you to

- Technical support on our customer hotline.
- Favored customer status.
- *Keywords*—the SPSS user newsletter.
- New product announcements.

Of course, unregistered systems receive none of the above, so *don't put it off—send your registration card now!*

Replacement Policy. Call the Micro Software Department at 312/329-3300 to report a defective diskette. You must provide us with the serial number of your system. SPSS Inc. will ship replacement diskettes the same day we receive notification from you. Please return the defective diskettes to the Micro Software Department, SPSS Inc., 444 North Michigan Avenue, Chicago, IL 60611, or to the SPSS International office nearest you.

Note: If you have installation problems, please call Technical Support before assuming your diskettes are defective.

Training Seminars. SPSS Inc. provides both public and onsite training seminars for SPSS for the Macintosh. There is an introductory course to familiarize users with the basics of SPSS for the Macintosh, and an advanced course. Additional seminars cover specialized topics. All seminars feature hands-on workshops.

SPSS for the Macintosh seminars will be offered in major U.S. and European cities on a regular basis. For further information on these seminars or to schedule an onsite seminar, call the SPSS Inc. Training Department at 312/329-2400.

Additional Documentation. Additional copies of all SPSS product manuals may be purchased separately. To order additional manuals, just fill out the Documentation Card included with your system and send it to SPSS Inc. Documentation Sales, 444 N. Michigan Avenue, Chicago, IL, 60611.

Note: In Europe, additional copies of documentation can be purchased by site-licensed customers only. Please contact the SPSS International office at the address listed on the copyright page for more information.

Technical Support. The SPSS technical hotline is available to registered customers of SPSS for the Macintosh. Customers may call Technical Support for assistance in using SPSS products or for installation help for one of the warranted hardware environments.

To reach a Technical Support consultant, call 312/329-3410, 9:00 a.m. to 5:00 p.m. CST. Be prepared to identify yourself, your organization, and the serial number of your system.

If you are a Value Plus or Customer EXPress customer, use the priority 800 number you received with your materials. For information on subscribing to the Value Plus or Customer EXPress plan, call SPSS Inc. at 312/329-3313.

Lend Us Your Thoughts. Your comments are important. So send us a letter and let us know about your experiences with SPSS products. We especially like to hear about new and interesting applications using the SPSS for the Macintosh system. Write to SPSS Inc. Marketing Department, Attn: Micro Software Products Manager, 444 N. Michigan Avenue, Chicago, IL, 60611.

In Conclusion. The SPSS system is constantly undergoing enhancements. Additional information about your system, including any updates since the printing of the most current version of the manual, is included in a file named Read Me. You can read this file by double-clicking its icon after installing SPSS for the Macintosh.

If you would like to be on our mailing list and you did not buy your system directly from us, write to us at one of the addresses below. We will send you a copy of our newsletter and let you know about SPSS Inc. activities in your area.

United States and Canada

SPSS Inc.
444 North Michigan Avenue
Chicago, IL 60611
Tel: (312) 329-3500
Fax: (312) 329-3668

Federal systems

SPSS Federal Systems (U.S.)
12300 Twinbrook Parkway, Suite 600
Rockville, MD 20852
Tel: (301) 770-1961
Fax: (301) 881-6898

Latin America

SPSS Latin America
444 North Michigan Avenue
Chicago, IL 60611
Tel: (312) 329-3556
Fax: (312) 329-3558

Europe and the Middle East

SPSS International BV
P.O. Box 115
4200 AC Gorinchem
The Netherlands
Tel: +31.1830.36711
Twx: 21019
Fax: +31.1830.35839

United Kingdom,
Ireland, Israel, Africa

SPSS UK Ltd.
SPSS House
5 London Street
Chertsey, Surrey KT16 8AP
United Kingdom
Tel: +44.932.566262
Fax: +44.932.567020

Germany, Italy, Austria,
Switzerland, Eastern Europe

SPSS GmbH Software
Steinsdorfstrasse 19
D-8000 Munich
Federal Republic of Germany
Tel: +49.89.2283008
Twx: 082+ 5218457
Fax: +49.89.2285413

The Netherlands, Belgium, Luxembourg

SPSS Benelux BV
Gebouw Hagestein
Ir. D.S. Tuijnmanweg 2E
P.O. Box 54
4130 EB Vianen
The Netherlands
Tel: +31.3473.75706
Fax: +31.3473.73026

Sweden, Denmark, Norway, Finland

SPSS Scandinavia AB
Sjoangsvagen 21
S-19172 Sollentuna
Sweden
Tel: +46.8.7549450
Fax: +46.8.7548816

Asia Pacific

SPSS Asia Pacific Pte. Ltd.
26-01
78 Shenton Way
Singapore 0207
Singapore
Tel: +65.221.2577
Fax: +65.221.9920

Japan

SPSS Japan Inc.
Gyoen Sky Bldg.
2-1-11, Shinjuku
Tokyo 160
Japan
Tel: +81.3.350.5261
Fax: +81.3.350.5245

Australia, New Zealand

SPSS Australasia
P.O. Box 879
345 Pacific Highway
Crows Nest
Sydney, NSW 2065
Australia
Tel: +61.2.954.5660
Fax: +61.2.954.5616

Contents

SPSS for the Macintosh Documentation   1

MANUALS FOR THE BASE SYSTEM   2
INSTALLATION INSTRUCTIONS   2
MANUALS FOR THE ADD-ON OPTIONS   3
ONLINE DOCUMENTATION   3
IN THIS MANUAL   4

Overview: SPSS for the Macintosh   5

WHAT YOU SHOULD KNOW   5
INSTALLATION INSTRUCTIONS   6
FEATURES OF SPSS FOR THE MACINTOSH   6
    Two Sets of Menus   6
        Menu Bar   6
        Command Generator Menus   6

    Windows for Input and Output   8
    Data Files   8
        Variable Names   9

    Context-Sensitive Information   9
A TYPICAL SPSS SESSION   9
COMMANDS THAT ARE NOT IN SPSS FOR THE MACINTOSH   14
COMMANDS UNIQUE TO SPSS FOR THE MACINTOSH   14
SETTINGS UNIQUE TO SPSS FOR THE MACINTOSH   14
NAMES OF KEYS   14
TERMINOLOGY USED IN DIFFERENT CONTEXTS   15
NOTE TO SPSS/PC+ USERS   15
    Procedure Commands   15
    Transformation and Utility Commands   16
    SPSS/PC+ System Files   17
    Matrix Materials   17
    Beginning and Ending an SPSS Session   17
        Beginning a Session   17
        Ending a Session   18

Chapter 1 **Entering SPSS Commands 19**

 1.1 BEGIN AN SPSS SESSION 19
 1.2 GET AN SPSS SYSTEM FILE 21
 1.3 ENTER COMMANDS WITH THE COMMAND GENERATOR 23
   1.4 Make Selections 23
   1.5 Paste Commands 24
   1.6 Type in Specifications 26
 1.7 RUN A COMMAND 26
 1.8 DISPLAY LABELS IN THE VARIABLES WINDOW 28
 1.9 PERFORM AN ANALYSIS 30
 1.10 VIEW THE OUTPUT 32
 1.11 PRACTICE 32
 1.12 END AN SPSS SESSION 33
   1.13 Save the Input Window as a Command File 33
 1.14 SUMMARY 34

Chapter 2 **Using SPSS Command Files 35**

 2.1 OPEN AN SPSS COMMAND FILE 35
 2.2 MODIFY AND RUN COMMANDS 37
   2.3 Set the Directory 37
   2.4 Type a New Command 37
   2.5 Run the Commands 38
   2.6 Add More Commands 39
 2.7 SAVE THE COMMAND FILE 40
 2.8 RUNNING COMMANDS FROM A DIFFERENT COMMAND FILE 41
 2.9 PRACTICE 42
 2.10 SUMMARY 43

Chapter R1 **SPSS Menus and Windows 44**

 R1.1 APPLE MENU 45
   R1.2 About SPSS 45
 R1.3 FILE MENU 45
   R1.4 New 46
   R1.5 Open 46
   R1.6 Close 47
   R1.7 Save 47
   R1.8 Save As 48
   R1.9 Append Window or Append Selection 48
   R1.10 Get SPSS System File 48
   R1.11 Save SPSS System File 48
   R1.12 Get Data File 49
   R1.13 Save Data File 50
   R1.14 Page Setup 50
   R1.15 Print Window 50

R1.16 Print Selection   51
R1.17 Set Directory   51
R1.18 Quit   52

R1.19 EDIT MENU   52

R1.20 Undo   54
R1.21 Redo   54
R1.22 Cut   54
R1.23 Copy   54
R1.24 Paste   54
R1.25 Clear   55
R1.26 Copy Table   55
R1.27 Round   55
R1.28 Select Commands (in the Input Window)   56
R1.29 Select Lines (in the Output Window)   56
R1.30 Preferences   56

R1.31 SEARCH MENU   58

R1.32 Find   58
R1.33 Search and Replace   60

R1.34 RUN MENU   60

R1.35 WINDOW MENU   61

R1.36 Arrange All   62
R1.37 Command Generator   62
R1.38 Glossary Window   62
R1.39 Requesting Definitions   63
R1.40 Pasting Definitions into the Active Window   64
R1.41 Closing the Glossary Window   64

R1.42 Variables Window   64
R1.43 Looking Up Variable Names and Labels   66
R1.44 Selecting Variable Names for Pasting   66
R1.45 Pasting Variable Names   67

R1.46 Clipboard Window   67
R1.47 Output Window   67
R1.48 Input Window   68

R1.49 HELP MENU   68

Chapter R2   **Running SPSS for the Macintosh   70**

R2.1   BEGINNING AN SPSS SESSION   70

R2.2   Customizing the Session   71
R2.3 Workspace   71
R2.4 Rearrangement of Windows   71
R2.5 Window Width   72
R2.6 Storage of Temporary Files   72
R2.7 Closing the Preferences Box   72

R2.8   COMMANDS   72

R2.9   Entering Commands   73
R2.10 Navigating Command Generator Menus   73
R2.11 Pasting Selections   75
R2.12 Typing Commands   76
R2.13 Loading Commands from a File   76

R2.14 Running the Commands 77
R2.15 Interrupting Commands That Are Running 78

R2.16 Viewing and Editing Output 78
R2.17 COMMAND FILES 78
R2.18 Creating New Command Files 78
R2.19 Opening Existing Command Files 79
R2.20 Opening a Command File during an SPSS Session 79
R2.21 Opening a Command File from the Desktop 79

R2.22 Saving Command Files 79
R2.23 DATA FILES 80
R2.24 Getting Data Files 80
R2.25 Getting SPSS System Files 81
R2.26 Getting Other Data Files 81

R2.27 Reading Raw Data Files 83
R2.28 Reading Fixed Record-Length or Multipunch Files 84
R2.29 Saving Data Files 85
R2.30 Saving SPSS System Files 85
R2.31 Saving Other Data Files 86

R2.32 Referring to Files on SPSS Commands 87
R2.33 HELP 89
R2.34 Help for SPSS 89
R2.35 Online Syntax Charts 89

R2.36 SPSS Command Descriptions and Examples 89
R2.37 OUTPUT (LISTING) FILES 90
R2.38 Creating Listing Files 90
R2.39 Opening Listing Files 90
R2.40 Saving Output into Listing Files 90
R2.41 QUITTING A SESSION 91
R2.42 SELECTING OR SAVING FILES 91
R2.43 Types of Files 91
R2.44 Directory Dialog Boxes 92
R2.45 Directory Title 93
R2.46 Directory Contents 93
R2.47 Current Disk Name 94
R2.48 Buttons 94

R2.49 Selecting and Opening a File 94
R2.50 Saving a File 94
R2.51 Setting the Directory 95

Chapter R3   Text Editing in SPSS 97

R3.1   USING THE INSERTION POINT 97
    R3.2 Moving the Insertion Point with the Mouse 97
    R3.3 Moving the Insertion Point with Keyboard Keys 97

R3.4   EDITING TEXT 98
    R3.5 Adding New Lines 98
    R3.6 Appending Text to the End of a File 99
    R3.7 Copying Text 99
    R3.8 Deleting Text 100
    R3.9 Joining Lines 100
    R3.10 Moving Text 100
    R3.11 Pasting Definitions from the Glossary Window 100
    R3.12 Rounding Off Numbers 101
    R3.13 Splitting Lines 101
    R3.14 Typing Characters 101

R3.15 SELECTING TEXT 101
    R3.16 Selecting with the Edit Menu 102
        R3.17 Selecting Commands 102
        R3.18 Selecting Output Lines 102

    R3.19 Selecting with the Mouse 103
        R3.20 Selecting Lines 103
        R3.21 Selecting a Rectangular Area 103

    R3.22 Deselecting Text 103

Chapter R4   Exceptions to the SPSS Reference Guide 104

R4.1   SET SUBCOMMANDS WITH EXCEPTIONS 104
R4.2   ADDITIONAL SET SUBCOMMANDS 105
R4.3   SET SUBCOMMANDS NOT AVAILABLE 105
    R4.4 GRAPH Settings 105
    R4.5 Other Subcommands Not Available 105
R4.6   GET AND SAVE TRANSLATE KEYWORDS 105
R4.7   READ ME FILE VERSUS INFO COMMAND 106

Appendix A   Installation and Setup 107

A.1   INSTALLING SPSS FOR THE MACINTOSH 108
    A.2 Installing Additional Files 109
    A.3 Online Help 110
    A.4 Removing Installed Modules 110
    A.5 Preparing Other System Disks 110
    A.6 What Next? 111
A.7   USING SETUP AFTER SPSS HAS BEEN INSTALLED 111

A.8   Installing or Removing Optional Files   111
A.9 Starting Setup   111
A.10 Installing Files That Were Not Previously Installed   111
A.11 Installing SPSSfont   112
A.12 Removing Installed Files   113

A.13   Updating Installed Files   113

Appendix B   Important Macintosh Concepts   114

B.1   MANIPULATING WINDOWS   114
B.2   Closing a Window   115
B.3   Enlarging a Window   115
B.4   Moving a Window   115
B.5   Using the Keyboard to Move the Pointer   115
B.6   Scrolling a Window   115
B.7   PRINTING   116
B.8   Choosing Printing Features   116
B.9   ACTIVATING A BUTTON   117
B.10   RUNNING COMMANDS WITH THE ENTER KEY   117
B.11   WORKING IN MORE THAN ONE APPLICATION   117

Appendix C   Drawing Graphs with Cricket Graph   118

C.1   RUNNING CRICKET GRAPH   118
C.2   Running a Basic CRICKET Command   118
C.3   Draw a Graph   119
C.4   Examples   120
C.5 Line Graph   121
C.6 Pie Chart   123
C.7 Scatterplots   123
C.8 Histogram   126

C.9   CRICKET COMMAND REFERENCE   126
C.10   Syntax   126
C.11   Overview   127
C.12   Subcommand Order   128
C.13   Syntax Rules   128
C.14   Operations   128
C.15   Limitations   129
C.16   Examples   129
C.17   TABLE Subcommand   129
C.18 Histograms   130
C.19 TABLE Functions   130

C.20   CASEFILE Subcommand   131

Appendix D   Variable Format Types 133

D.1   INPUT AND OUTPUT FORMATS 133

    D.2   Printable Numeric Formats 137

        D.3 Fw.d (Standard Numeric) 137
        D.4 Nw.d (Restricted Numeric) 138
        D.5 Ew.d (Scientific Notation) 138
        D.6 COMMAw.d (Commas in Numbers) 139
        D.7 DOTw.d (Dots in Numbers) 139
        D.8 DOLLARw.d (Dollar Sign and Commas in Numbers) 139
        D.9 PCTw.d (Percent Sign after Numbers) 140
        D.10 PIBHEXw (Hexadecimal of PIB) 140
        D.11 RBHEXw (Hexadecimal of RB) 140
        D.12 Zw.d (Zoned Decimal) 141

    D.13 Nonprintable Numeric Input Formats 141

        D.14 IBw.d (Integer Binary) 142
        D.15 PIBw.d (Positive Integer Binary) 142
        D.16 Pw.d (Packed Decimal) 142
        D.17 PKw.d (Unsigned Packed Decimal) 142
        D.18 RBw (Real Binary) 143

    D.19 String Formats 143

        D.20 Aw (Standard Characters) 143
        D.21 AHEXw (Hexadecimal Characters) 143

    D.22 Date and Time Input Formats 143

        D.23 DATE 144
        D.24 ADATEw (American Date) 144
        D.25 JDATEw (Julian Date) 144
        D.26 QYRw (Quarter and Year) 145
        D.27 MOYRw (Month and Year) 145
        D.28 WKYRw (Week and Year) 145
        D.29 TIMEw (Time) 145
        D.30 DTIMEw (Days and Time) 146
        D.31 DATETIMEw (Date and Time) 146
        D.32 WKDAYw (Day of the Week) 146
        D.33 MONTHw (Month) 147

D.34 T AND X FORMAT ELEMENTS 147

D.35 COLUMN BINARY FORMAT 148

    D.36 Limitations 149
    D.37 Column Binary Data on Disk 150

D.38 UNALIGNED POSITIVE INTEGER BINARY FORMAT 151

    D.39 UPIB versus Column Binary Format 151
    D.40 Limitations 151

Index 153

SPSS for the Macintosh Documentation

SPSS statistical software runs on many different computers and operating systems. SPSS uses the same basic commands in all systems (exceptions for the Macintosh are noted in this manual), but the way you build and submit commands differs from system to system. Thus, you need this book to learn how to build commands and interact with SPSS on the Macintosh. You need additional manuals (discussed below) to learn about the types of analyses you can perform with SPSS, and to learn the SPSS commands you can use to perform them.

SPSS software available for the Macintosh consists of the base system and four add-on options:

- SPSS Advanced Statistics.
- SPSS Trends.
- SPSS Tables.
- SPSS Categories.

The following sections discuss the manuals you need to operate each of these systems.

MANUALS FOR THE BASE SYSTEM

The base system in SPSS for the Macintosh contains all the commands and utilities you need to read and manage your data. It also contains the commands you need to perform basic statistical analyses.

The following manuals come with the base system:

- *SPSS Base System User's Guide* is a guide to analyzing data using the commands available in the base system of SPSS. It explains many of the statistical concepts involved and provides a brief discussion of the options available for each command. Its primary emphasis is statistical; it does not explore SPSS commands in full detail.
- *SPSS Reference Guide* provides a complete and detailed reference to all SPSS commands, subcommands, and keywords in the base system and Advanced Statistics option. It also contains the universal rules that apply to all SPSS commands and includes many examples.
- *SPSS for the Macintosh: Operations Guide* tells you how to run SPSS in a Macintosh operating system, including information on how to begin and end an SPSS session; create, open, or save files; build and run commands; browse and edit output; and get online help. This manual is outlined in more detail below.

The *SPSS Base System User's Guide* and *SPSS Reference Guide* apply to SPSS on all operating systems. These manuals discuss statistical concepts and the syntax for SPSS commands. They tell you which commands you need to perform various analyses. They do not tell you how to build or run those commands in SPSS for the Macintosh, or for any other operating system. They simply provide examples you can use as models for forming your own commands.

The *SPSS for the Macintosh: Operations Guide* applies only to the Macintosh operating system. It tells you how to get your data, how to use files and generate commands, and how to save output. It does not teach you statistics or the syntax of SPSS commands. To learn about statistics or the SPSS commands needed to obtain those statistics, refer to the *SPSS Base System User's Guide* and the *SPSS Reference Guide.*

INSTALLATION INSTRUCTIONS

Installation instructions for SPSS for the Macintosh are in Appendix A.

MANUALS FOR THE ADD-ON OPTIONS

To perform advanced statistical analyses, to forecast future trends using time series analysis, to format your data into tables for formal presentation, or to perform conjoint analysis and optimal scaling, you need one or more add-on options to SPSS for the Macintosh. Each add-on option comes with its own manual. As with the *SPSS Base System User's Guide* and the *SPSS Reference Guide,* manuals for the add-on options are written for all operating systems.

Manuals for the add-on options are:

- *SPSS Advanced Statistics User's Guide* contains discussions of advanced statistical analyses, such as discriminant analysis, nonlinear and logistic regression analysis, and multivariate analysis of variance. In addition to the statistical discussions, there is a brief discussion of how to run each command. The complete reference for the commands in the Advanced Statistics option is included in the *SPSS Reference Guide,* which comes with the base system.

- *SPSS Trends* documents SPSS's complete time series analysis and forecasting tool. The Trends option includes curve-fitting, smoothing, special regression, seasonal adjustment, and Box-Jenkins/ARIMA modeling procedures. A complete reference to commands in the Trends option is included in this manual.

- *SPSS Tables* documents the SPSS TABLES procedure, which produces presentation-quality tables. TABLES can tabulate multiple variables at once and provides great flexibility for displaying totals, percentages, and other statistics. The *SPSS Tables* manual includes a user's guide for TABLES and a complete reference to TABLES subcommands.

- *SPSS Categories* documents SPSS's conjoint and optimal scaling procedures. The Categories option includes procedures for developing conjoint studies and analyzing conjoint results. It also provides four procedures for optimal scaling, including correspondence analysis. A user's guide and a complete command reference for the Categories option are included.

ONLINE DOCUMENTATION

When you install the SPSS system, a Read Me file is installed in your SPSS 4.0 folder. The file type is TEXT, which can be opened by most word-processing applications and by SPSS itself. The Read Me file contains information about changes and additions to SPSS since the manuals were printed.

SPSS for the Macintosh also includes a help system, glossary system, and command descriptions. All are mentioned in Overview: SPSS for the Macintosh (next chapter) and are discussed in detail in Chapters R1 and R2.

IN THIS MANUAL

This manual is organized into the following sections:

Overview. The Overview

- Tells you what manuals and online documentation are available for SPSS for the Macintosh.
- Tells about features of SPSS for the Macintosh.
- Tells you which of the commands that are documented in the *SPSS Reference Guide* are not available in SPSS for the Macintosh.
- Briefly describes a typical SPSS session.

Tutorials.

- **Chapter 1** tells you how to begin an SPSS session and how to use the menu system for entering commands.
- **Chapter 2** teaches you to use existing command files and also to type commands rather than enter them through the menus.

References.

- **Chapter R1** provides a reference to the menus.
- **Chapter R2** provides a reference to performing SPSS tasks.
- **Chapter R3** provides a reference to the SPSS editing capabilities.
- **Chapter R4** discusses the subcommands for the SET command that were added to SPSS for the Macintosh; that are not available in SPSS for the Macintosh; or that have exceptions to the way they are documented in the *SPSS Reference Guide.*

Appendixes.

- **Appendix A** tells you how to install SPSS for the Macintosh on your computer, using the SPSS Setup program. It also tells you how to use Setup after installation to install additional files, remove optional files that have already been installed, and update installed files if you purchase new versions of SPSS for the Macintosh programs.
- **Appendix B** discusses some Macintosh features as they apply to SPSS.
- **Appendix C** teaches you how to set up and transport your SPSS data for display in Cricket Graph™.
- **Appendix D** defines the data formats available in SPSS for the Macintosh.

Overview: SPSS for the Macintosh

SPSS for the Macintosh runs the same statistical procedures that are available in SPSS mainframe products. Through several generations of SPSS products, the procedures have been tested and refined to produce accurate, reliable results. In addition to the standard statistical procedures used for many years, SPSS for the Macintosh contains procedures incorporating recent developments in statistics.

To get a sense of how SPSS for the Macintosh works, read this overview, which contains a brief description of an SPSS session. Then, if you want step-by-step instructions, follow the tutorials in Chapters 1 and 2, which use data files you received with SPSS for the Macintosh. After that you will be ready to perform analyses using data of your own and commands modeled after the examples shown in the *SPSS Base System User's Guide* and *SPSS Reference Guide*.

WHAT YOU SHOULD KNOW

To use SPSS for the Macintosh effectively, you should be acquainted with the concepts of the Finder, the desktop, and simple editing. The quickest way to learn the Finder is to go through the tutorials in the *Macintosh System Software User's Guide.* You should be familiar with

- Using a mouse.
- Making windows active.
- Moving and sizing windows.
- Scrolling through windows.
- Choosing commands from menus.
- Cut, Copy, and Paste commands.

For more information on the application of Macintosh concepts in SPSS, see Appendix B of this manual.

INSTALLATION INSTRUCTIONS

You can find instructions on how to install SPSS for the Macintosh in Appendix A of this manual.

FEATURES OF SPSS FOR THE MACINTOSH

SPSS for the Macintosh uses Macintosh tools to help you gain access to SPSS statistical procedures. The menus allow you to explore and choose the specific data and analyses you need. Information about all of the facilities is readily available online.

Two Sets of Menus

SPSS for the Macintosh displays two sets of menus: standard Macintosh menus on the menu bar for managing the session, and special SPSS menus in the Command Generator window for manipulating data and calculating statistics.

Menu Bar

The menus on the menu bar help you get and save files, edit text, obtain information about statistics and SPSS commands, and run commands. Information on how to use the commands listed on these menus is available from the **Help** menu.

Command Generator Menus

The other set of menus is found in the SPSS Command Generator window, where you can explore and select SPSS commands for statistical procedures and transformations. These menus operate like a standard Macintosh directory dialog box, which you use for opening or saving files. Additional information about commands is available to the right of the menu list, where a special box displays definitions and examples of the commands and keywords.

Menu bar

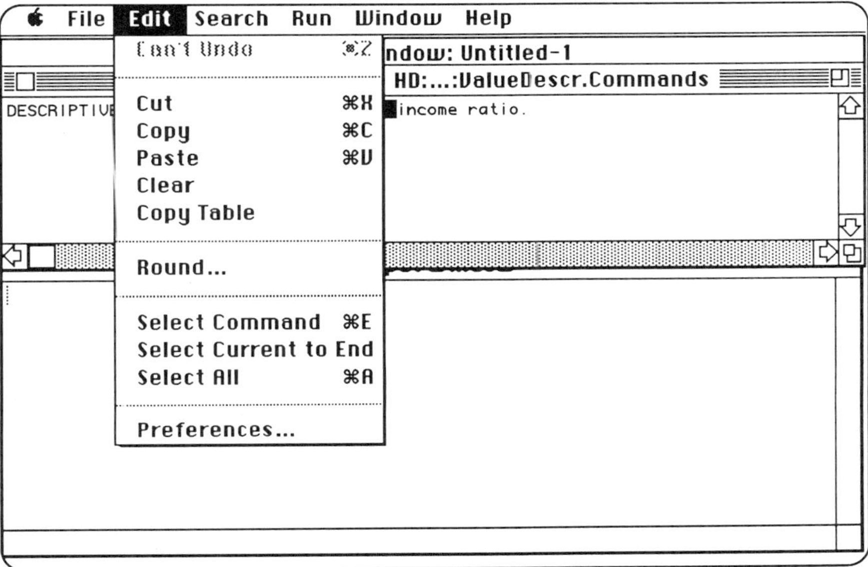

SPSS Command Generator menu

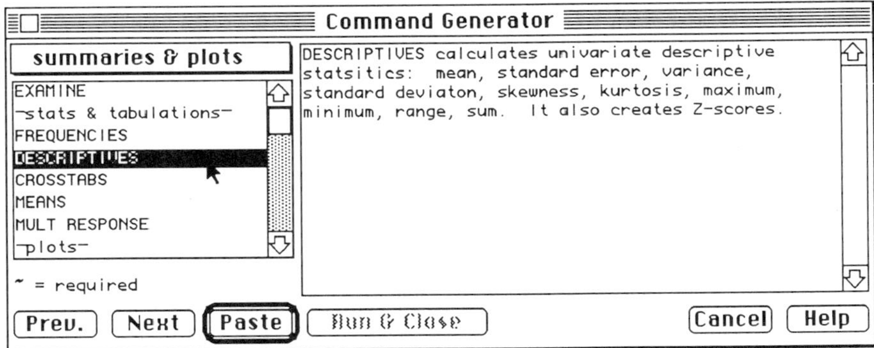

After you explore various subcommands and select appropriate ones, you can click the **Paste** button, and all the selected parts of the command are pasted into the Input window.

Windows for Input and Output

When running SPSS for the Macintosh, you enter commands for statistical procedures and data manipulation in the Input window and you view the results in the Output window.

Input and Output windows

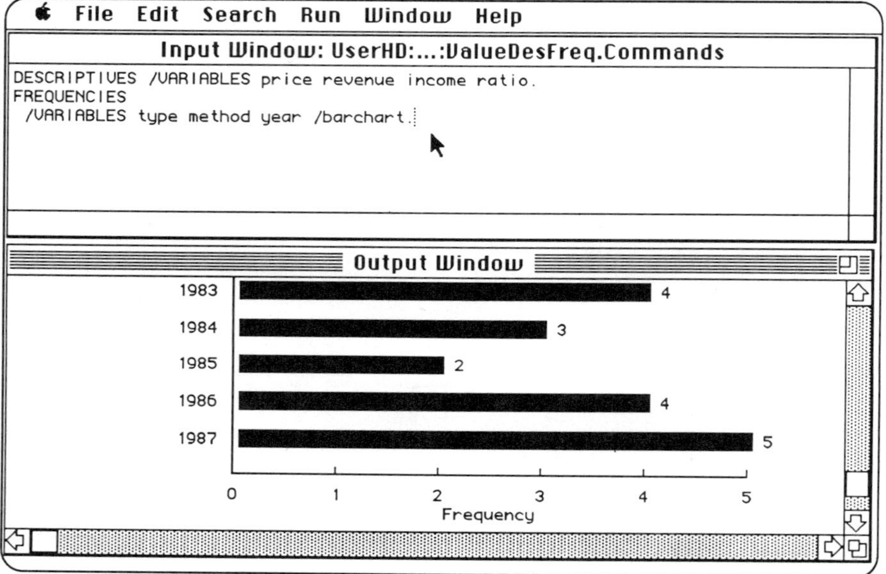

Data Files

The first requirement for statistical analysis is a set of data. The **File** menu has commands for getting many types of data files. After a data file has been brought in to SPSS for the Macintosh, you can save it in the SPSS system file format or another format.

Data files for SPSS can be created in several ways. You can

- Enter data in a spreadsheet or database application (for example, Excel or Multiplan), saving the file as a SYLK file, Text Only file, or tab-delimited file.

- Save a portable file in SPSS on another operating system, such as DOS or VAX/VMS, and then transport it to the Macintosh.

- Enter a "raw data" file in the SPSS Input window or in a word processor and then read it into SPSS with a command such as DATA LIST.

- Type or paste your data directly into a command file, between the BEGIN DATA and END DATA commands.

Variable Names

For efficient processing, names assigned to variables in SPSS are limited to eight characters. However, an expanded, easy-to-interpret label can be assigned to any variable for display in the output.

Context-Sensitive Information

You can access much of the information needed to run SPSS for the Macintosh right on your screen:

- A Read Me file on the Setup disk provides information that has become available since this book went to press. To access this information, double-click on its icon.
- For help with operations, use the **Help** menu. If you choose **Help** while a window or dialog box is active, the appropriate item is already selected.
- For definitions and examples of SPSS commands, choose **Command Generator** from the **Window** menu. If you open it while the insertion point is on a command in the Input window, the command and its definition appear immediately.
- For SPSS command syntax, use the **Help** menu and scroll to the second half of the list.
- For definitions of statistical terms, choose **Glossary Window** from the **Window** menu. If the insertion point is within text, the glossary opens to the nearest alphabetical match.
- For a list of variables in your active SPSS system file, choose **Variables Window** from the **Window** menu. Variable labels appear as you select variables on the list.

The Glossary window and the Help window can be left open while you run SPSS commands.

A TYPICAL SPSS SESSION

The following steps illustrate a typical SPSS session.

❶ **Open SPSS.** When you double-click the SPSS icon, the Input window and the Output window appear.

❷ **Get data.** The first thing you need for the session is a data file. Probably you have a system file created by SPSS or you have an Excel or Multiplan file. The quickest way to access one of these data files is to choose a GET command from the *File* menu.

Getting a data file for the analysis

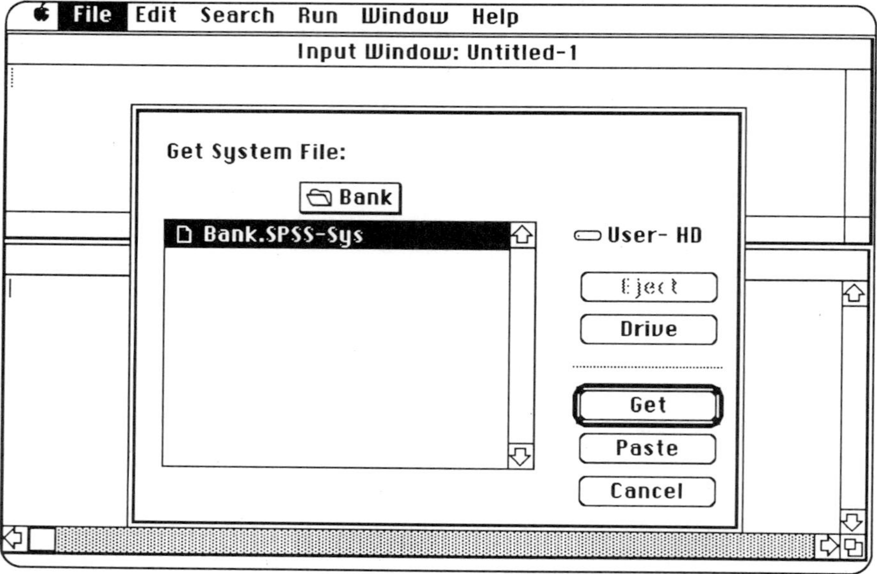

❸ **Generate SPSS commands.** Assume you have just been reading about the DE-SCRIPTIVES command in the *SPSS Base System User's Guide* and you want to obtain descriptive statistics on your data. Type **descriptives** into the Input window and then open the Command Generator window. Because the Command Generator is context sensitive, it opens at the subcommand level for DESCRIPTIVES.

❹ **Choose variables.** You observe that the VARIABLES subcommand is required (as indicated by the tilde ~), so you select it from the menu and *paste* it into the Input window. SPSS automatically opens the Variables window, which displays all the variables in your data. You select the variables you want to analyze.

Subcommands for the DESCRIPTIVES command

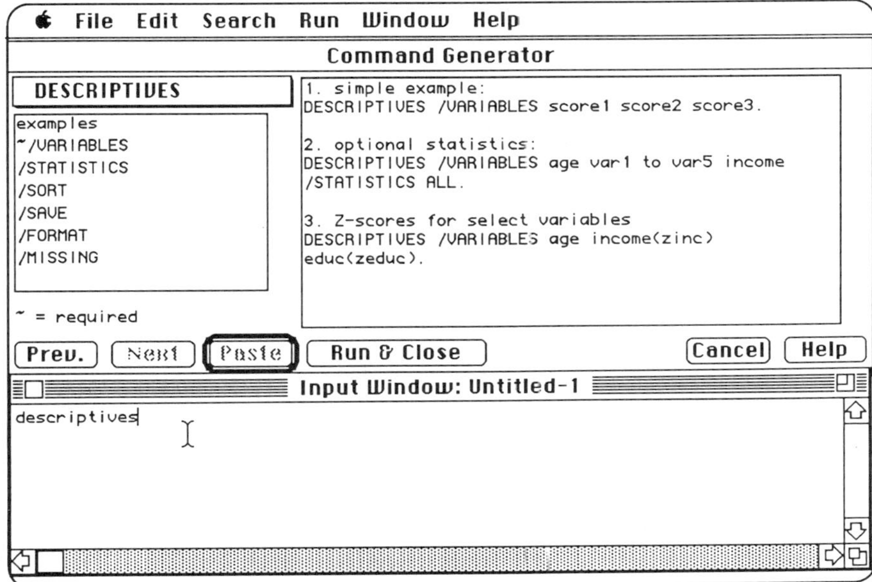

Variables selected for the analysis

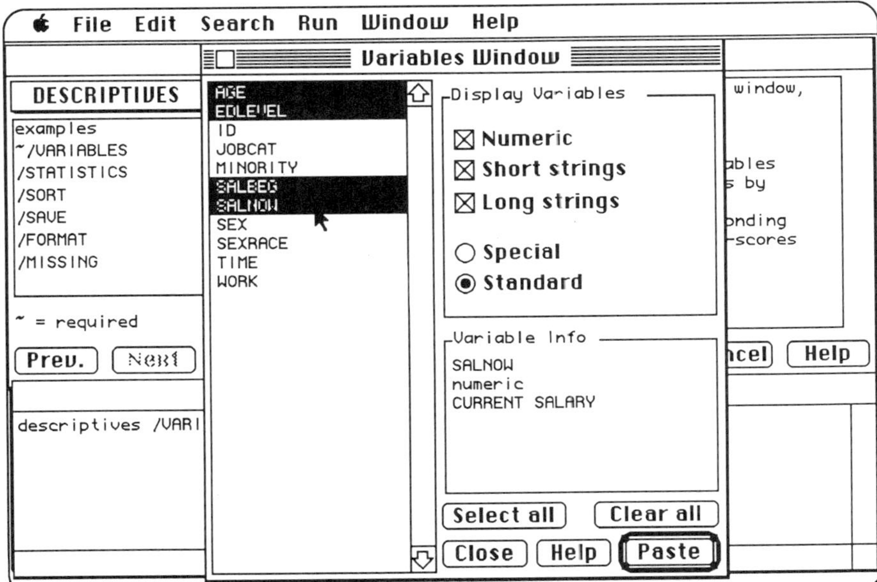

❺ Paste the variables. Click the **Paste** button to paste the variables into the Input window.

Pasted variable names

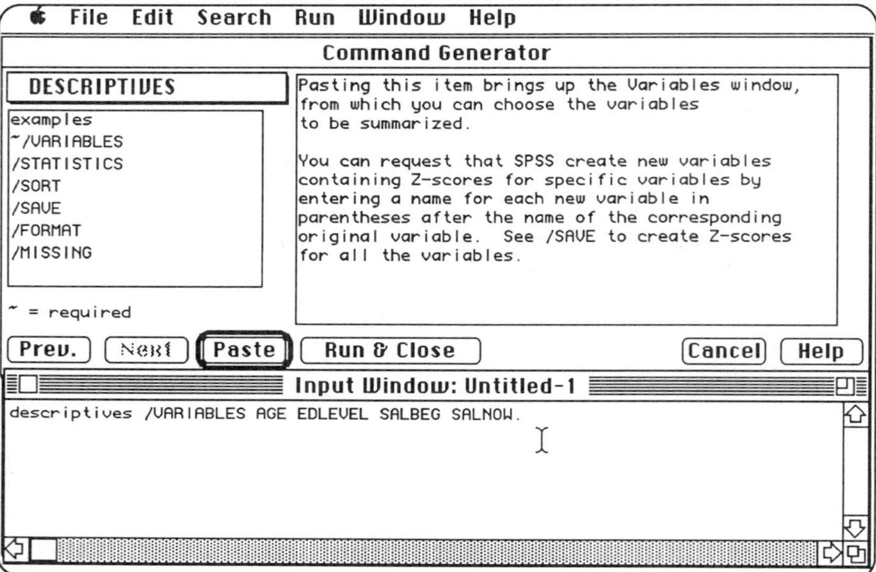

❻ Check the syntax. Choose **Help** from the **Help** menu and scroll down past the definitions to the syntax charts. Then click the DESCRIPTIVES command.

Online syntax chart

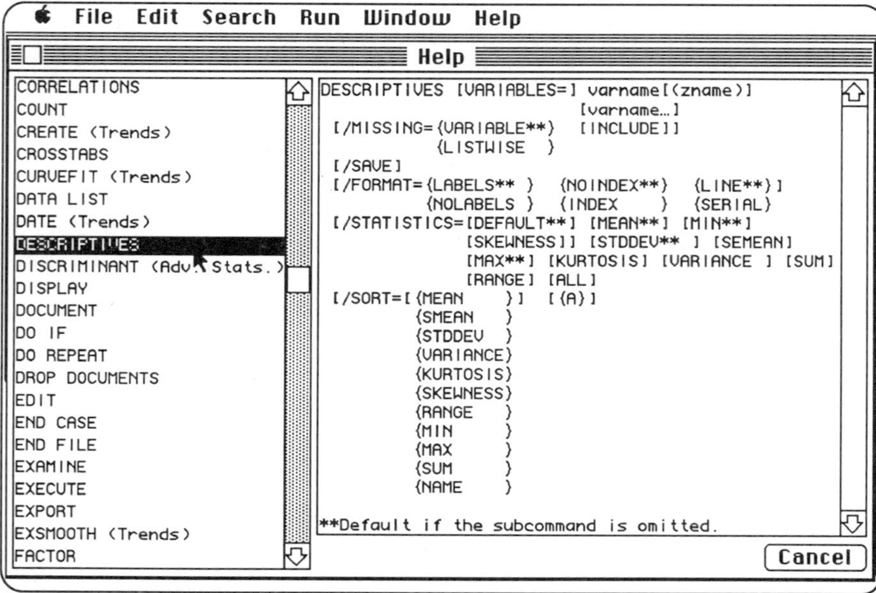

By looking at the chart, you determine that you have met the syntax requirements for building a basic DESCRIPTIVES command.

❼ Run the command. You click **Run & Close.** The status box appears with a spinning beachball. SPSS executes the DESCRIPTIVES command and begins sending results and messages to the Output window.

❽ View the output. Click in the Output window and study your output. Then select and save a relevant portion of it.

Selected portions of output to save

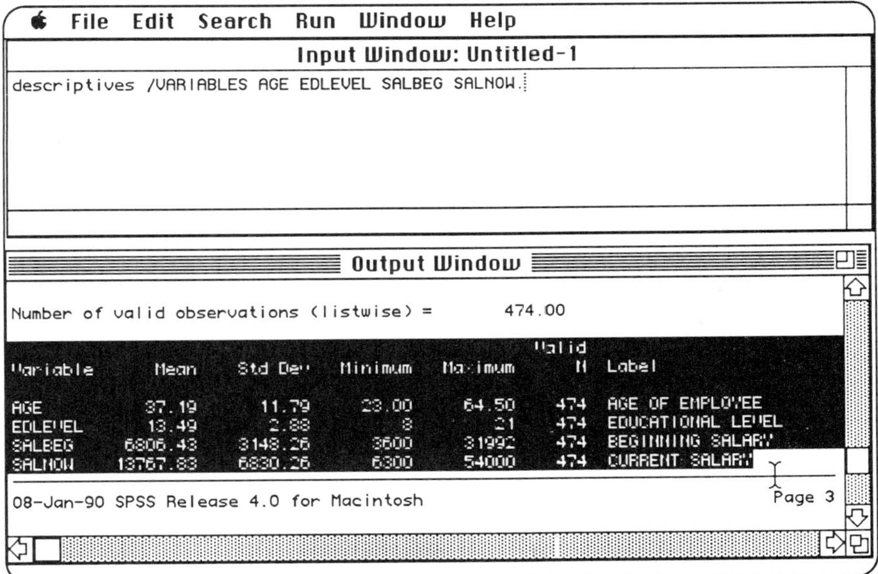

Variable	Mean	Std Dev	Minimum	Maximum	Valid N	Label
AGE	37.19	11.79	23.00	64.50	474	AGE OF EMPLOYEE
EDLEVEL	13.49	2.88	8	21	474	EDUCATIONAL LEVEL
SALBEG	6806.43	3148.26	3600	31992	474	BEGINNING SALARY
SALNOW	13767.83	6830.26	6300	54000	474	CURRENT SALARY

❾ Enter and run more commands. You return to the Input window, enter several more commands, and then run them as a block.

❿ Use another application. Rather than continue working in SPSS, you decide to let SPSS churn away (while the beachball is spinning) and use another application. (To do this, you need a Macintosh with about 4MB of memory.) With the MultiFinder on, you click the icons in the upper right corner of the menu bar and cycle through open applications until you reach the application you want. This does not affect your SPSS session. The session is still active, and SPSS continues to send output to the Output window. If SPSS finishes before you return to the session, it remains in a ready state.

⓫ Return to SPSS. When you are ready, return to SPSS, scroll through the Output window, and save the output file for later use.

⓬ Quit SPSS. To end the session, choose **Quit** from the **File** menu.

COMMANDS THAT ARE NOT IN SPSS FOR THE MACINTOSH

The following commands that are documented in the *SPSS Reference Guide* are not available in SPSS for the Macintosh:

- GET BMDP
- GET OSIRIS
- GET SAS
- GET SCSS and SAVE SCSS
- GRAPH
- HOST
- INFO
- KEYED DATA LIST
- POINT

COMMANDS UNIQUE TO SPSS FOR THE MACINTOSH

The CRICKET command uses SPSS data to generate files in Cricket Graph format. If Cricket Graph is installed, you can then use it to draw a variety of charts. The CRICKET command is described in Appendix C.

SETTINGS UNIQUE TO SPSS FOR THE MACINTOSH

Chapter R4 describes

- SET subcommands that are not available in SPSS for the Macintosh.
- SET subcommands in SPSS for the Macintosh that have exceptions to the way they are documented in the *SPSS Reference Guide.*
- SET subcommands that were added to SPSS for the Macintosh.

NAMES OF KEYS

Several different keyboards are available for the Macintosh. When this manual refers to the "delete" key, you can use the key labeled "backspace" on a Macintosh Plus keyboard.

TERMINOLOGY USED IN DIFFERENT CONTEXTS

document   Applications on the Macintosh create documents. The term document in this context refers to a file that you can open and edit. In another context, SPSS has a DOCUMENT command that enables you to save a block of text within an SPSS system file, which contains data and a dictionary that defines the data. Usually information created with the DOCUMENT command contains descriptive information about the file and its variables. This text can later be displayed in the Output window or dropped from the SPSS system file.

system file   The System Folder on the Macintosh has *system files* that contain operating information for the Macintosh. SPSS for the Macintosh generates a special type of file called an *SPSS system file*. Each SPSS system file contains data and a dictionary describing that data, all in a special format that SPSS can read quickly. On the **File** menu are the commands **Get SPSS System File** and **Save SPSS System File**, referring to these special files.

command   SPSS for the Macintosh contains a menu bar, like other Macintosh applications. On the menus are *commands* that initate various computer operations when you select them. For analyzing data, SPSS has another set of commands that you can either create with the Command Generator or type into the Input window.

menu   As described earlier in this overview, SPSS has two types of menus: those found on the menu bar and those found in the SPSS Command Generator.

NOTE TO SPSS/PC+ USERS

If you are an experienced SPSS/PC+ user, you will quickly learn SPSS for the Macintosh. However, you must be aware that SPSS for the Macintosh *is not* an enhanced version of SPSS/PC+; rather, it is a version of SPSS's mainframe product that runs on the Macintosh systems. This means that most of your existing SPSS/PC+ command files will not run in SPSS for the Macintosh unless you edit them. The modifications generally will be minor. By comparing the syntax diagram for a command in SPSS/PC+ with its syntax diagram in SPSS for the Macintosh, you should quickly discover the differences.

Procedure Commands

All the statistical procedures that are in SPSS/PC+ are also in SPSS for the Macintosh. In SPSS for the Macintosh, many have more capabilities, but they also use slightly different syntax—a syntax that is easier to use and to remember.

Two notable differences are

- OPTIONS and STATISTICS subcommands. None of the procedure commands in SPSS for the Macintosh use OPTIONS subcommands or specify only numbers on a STATISTICS subcommand. For example, the SPSS/PC+ command

```
DESCRIPTIVES VARIABLES=PRICE RATIO
 /OPTION=3
 /STATISTICS=1,6.
```

is

```
DESCRIPTIVES VARIABLES=PRICE RATIO
 /SAVE
 /STATISTICS=MEAN VARIANCE.
```

in SPSS for the Macintosh.

To see a cross-reference of the changes from SPSS/PC+ OPTIONS and STATISTICS numbers to SPSS subcommands and keywords, refer to the appendix for obsolete commands in the *SPSS Reference Guide.*

- The SPSS/PC+ command DSCRIMINANT is spelled DISCRIMINANT in SPSS for the Macintosh.

Transformation and Utility Commands

The following SPSS/PC+ commands do not exist but have equivalents in SPSS for the Macintosh.

- JOIN. The join function in SPSS for the Macintosh is performed by two separate commands: ADD FILES and MATCH FILES. SPSS for the Macintosh also has an UPDATE command so you can update existing system files.
- PROCESS IF. In SPSS for the Macintosh, the TEMPORARY command controls temporary transformations. TEMPORARY has broader application than PROCESS IF.
- TRANSLATE. Two separate commands in SPSS for the Macintosh are used to translate foreign files: GET TRANSLATE and SAVE TRANSLATE.

The following SPSS/PC+ commands do not exist in SPSS for the Macintosh:

- MODIFY VARIABLES.
- REVIEW.
- SPSS MANAGER.
- SYSFILE INFO.

SPSS/PC+ System Files

SPSS for the Macintosh cannot read system files created in SPSS/PC+. To read an SPSS/PC+ system file, you must write it out from SPSS/PC+ as a *portable* file with the EXPORT command. In addition, SPSS for the Macintosh *cannot* save a system file in SPSS/PC+ format. To read a data file created by SPSS for the Macintosh in SPSS/PC+, you must save the file as a portable file with the EXPORT command in SPSS for the Macintosh and read it with the IMPORT command in SPSS/PC+. To save the portable file, choose **Save Data File** from the **File** menu and then choose **Portable**.

Matrix Materials

Commands in SPSS/PC+ that handle matrix materials (CLUSTER, CORRELA-TIONS, FACTOR, MANOVA, ONEWAY, and REGRESSION) read and write them in ASCII format. In SPSS for the Macintosh, matrix materials are formatted as system files.

To read matrix materials from SPSS/PC+, you must use the MATRIX DATA command. You can then read the matrix into the appropriate procedure or save it as an SPSS matrix system file. See the *SPSS Reference Guide* for more information about matrix system files.

Beginning and Ending an SPSS Session

There are slight differences in the way SPSS/PC+ and SPSS for the Macintosh begin and end a session.

Beginning a Session

In SPSS/PC+ you begin a session by issuing the SPSSPC command at the DOS prompt. If you specify the name of a command file on the SPSSPC command, the file must contain a GET, IMPORT, JOIN, TRANSLATE, or DATA LIST command to define data for the session. Commands in the file are then executed automatically.

In SPSS for the Macintosh, you begin a session by opening SPSS from the desktop, or by double-clicking an SPSS file. If you double-click a command file, it does not have to contain a command to define data for the session. However, before you can run any of the commands in such a file, you must get a data file by using the **File** menu or enter and run a command that defines data for the session.

Ending a Session

In SPSS/PC+, if you use (F10) to open the **run** menu and then choose **Exit to prompt,** your session is still active and you go to the **SPSS/PC** prompt.

In SPSS for the Macintosh, if you choose **Quit** from the **File** menu, you end the SPSS session.

Chapter 1

Entering SPSS Commands

This chapter shows you how to

- Begin an SPSS session.
- Get an SPSS system file.
- Enter commands using the SPSS Command Generator.
- Run a command.
- Display variable labels.
- Perform a simple analysis.
- End an SPSS session.

This tutorial uses data stored in the SPSS system file Bank.SPSS-Sys, which you received with SPSS for the Macintosh. It assumes that the files and folders are installed and named as suggested in the installation instructions (see Appendix A).

1.1 BEGIN AN SPSS SESSION

Your screen should resemble Figure 1.1a when you turn on your Macintosh. The appearance of the screen is the same as when you turned off your computer.

Figure 1.1a *Macintosh desktop*

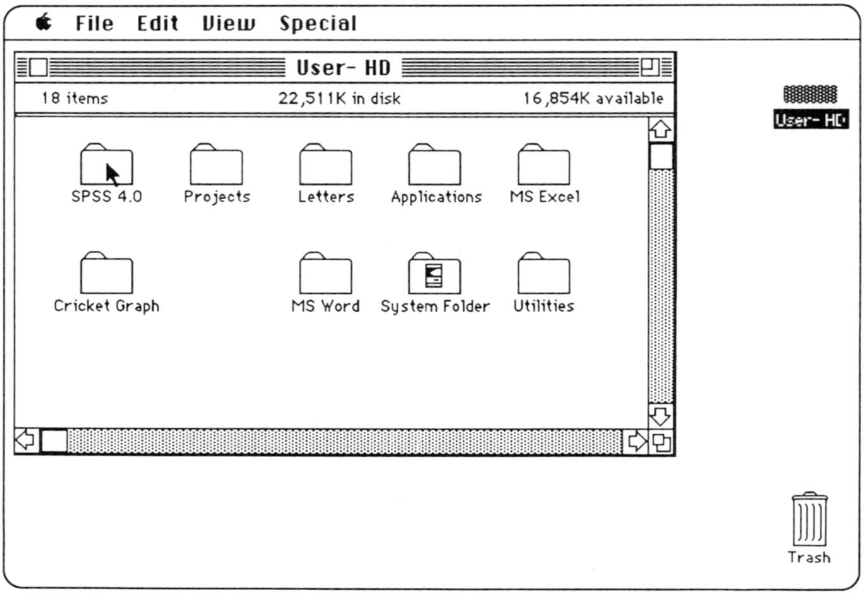

Follow these steps to start a session:

❶ Start at the directory for your hard disk.

❷ Click the **SPSS 4.0** folder to select it. (You may have to scroll the window to find it.)

❸ Move the pointer to the word **File** in the menu bar.

❹ Press and hold the mouse button to open the **File** menu.

❺ Drag the pointer to **Open** and release the mouse button. This chooses the **Open** command and opens the **SPSS 4.0** folder.

❻ Click the **SPSS** icon and choose **Open** from the **File** menu (or double-click the SPSS icon). This opens SPSS for the Macintosh and displays the logo screen.

After the logo, two windows and a dialog box appear:

Input window	You use this window to enter SPSS commands and specifications. It is empty when you begin.
Output window	SPSS uses this window to display output.
status dialog box	This dialog box appears in front of the windows. SPSS uses this box to report on session status. For example, it tells you whether the last command issued is running. It also provides other useful information, such as how many cases have been processed so far. For

example, Figure 1.1b shows a status dialog box during LIST command processing. When you begin a session, the status box displays the message **SPSS Working**. When SPSS is ready, the status box disappears.

Figure 1.1b *Status dialog box during LIST processing*

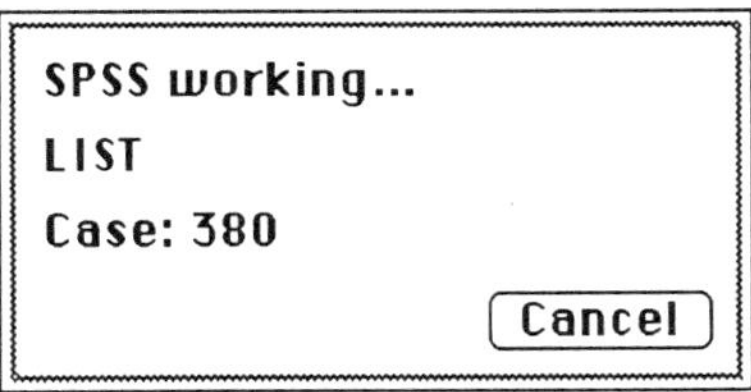

1.2 GET AN SPSS SYSTEM FILE

The first requirement for an analysis is data. To begin this tutorial you will get the SPSS system file Bank.SPSS-Sys which you received with SPSS for the Macintosh. This file contains data values plus descriptive information about those values.

To get the SPSS system file, follow these steps:

❶ Move the pointer to **File** in the menu bar and press the mouse button. This pulls down the **File** menu, as shown in Figure 1.2a.

Figure 1.2a *File menu*

❷ Choose **Get SPSS System File**. The **Get System File** directory dialog box appears, as shown in Figure 1.2b. In the list of files is a **Bank** folder. There may be other files also.

Figure 1.2b *Get System File dialog box*

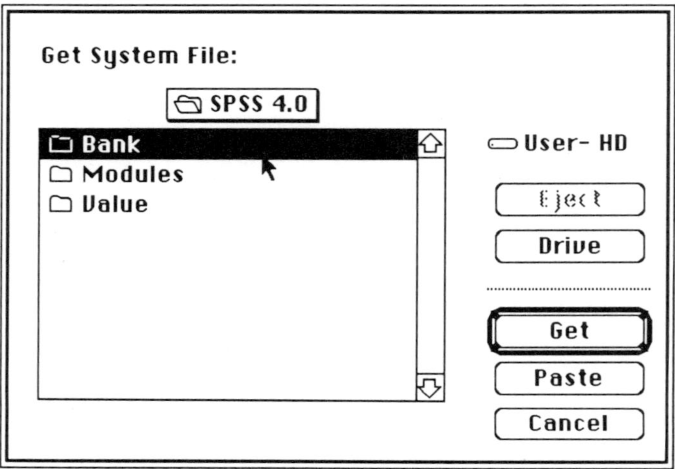

❸ Click the **Bank** folder to select it and then click the **Get** button. In the contents of the **Bank** folder is a document **Bank.SPSS-Sys**. If you have other system files, they are also listed.

❹ Move the pointer to the list of files and click **Bank.SPSS-Sys** to select the file. (It may already be selected.)

❺ Click the **Get** button to get the file you selected (or double-click).

The status dialog box opens and the pointer becomes a spinning beachball. This tells you SPSS is running the SPSS GET command, which gets an SPSS system file. When the SPSS system file is open, the status dialog box closes.

Now look in the Output window. The Output window shows the SPSS GET command, including the name of the file you selected with its pathname (disk name and folders). This confirms that the file is open. Your screen should resemble Figure 1.2c.

Figure 1.2c *Output window*

```
                          Output Window
┌──────────────────────────────────────────────────────────────────┐
04-Jan-90 SPSS Release 4.0 for Macintosh                    Page  1

->    GET FILE 'User- HD:SPSS 4.0:Bank:Bank.SPSS-Sys'.

File User- HD:SPSS 4.0:Bank:Bank.SPSS-Sys
   Created:   04-OCT-89 14:09:17 - 11 variables

->
```

1.3 ENTER COMMANDS WITH THE COMMAND GENERATOR

You are now ready to enter commands for the analysis. To enter commands, you use the *SPSS Command Generator,* which lets you select commands and then *paste* them into the Input window.

❶ Choose **Command Generator** from the **Window** menu. This opens the Command Generator window, which appears at the top of your screen. Below it is the Input window. The Output window is also open, behind the Command Generator window.

The Command Generator window, like a directory dialog box, contains a list box on the left that lets you make selections. It also has description window on the right that describes the current selection. Both boxes have vertical scroll bars.

1.4 Make Selections

When you first open the SPSS Command Generator window, the **SPSS Main Menu** is open in the list box, where the option **orientation** is highlighted. A description of the highlighted option is in the window on the right.

Assume you want to analyze your data by listing the first 10 cases.

❷ Click **analyze data.**

❸ Read the description in the description window to see what types of analyses are available. Among the descriptions is **Lists and reports**. This confirms that **analyze data** is the option you want from the **Main Menu.**

❹ Click **Next**. The menu under **analyze data** appears. The **summaries & plots** option is selected on the new menu, and the menu title above the list box tells you that **analyze data** is the selection you made to get to this menu. Your screen should resemble Figure 1.4a.

Figure 1.4a *Selections for analyzing data*

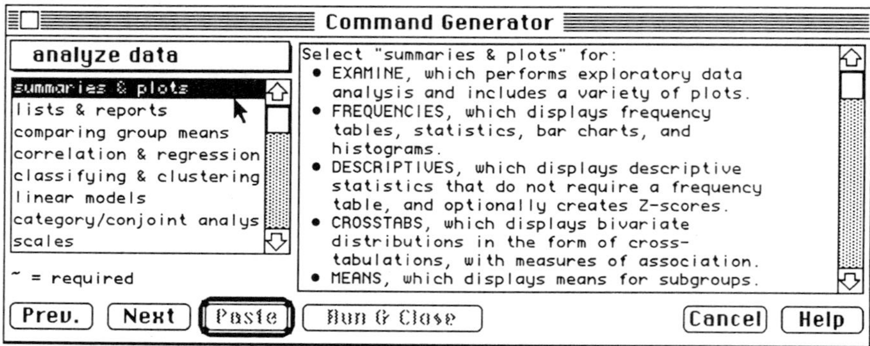

Note: If the options on your screen do not match those in Figure 1.4a, click the **Prev.** button, which returns you to the previous menu. (Even if your options match Figure 1.4a, click **Prev.** to see how it works. Then click **Next** to return to the screen that matches Figure 1.4a.)

❺ Click **lists & reports**.

❻ Read the description in the description window to see the commands available for generating lists and reports.

❼ Click **Next** (or double-click **lists & reports**).

1.5 Paste Commands

Your screen should resemble Figure 1.5a. Capitalized words in the menu on the left are commands, subcommands, and special keywords from SPSS's command language. From this menu, you can paste a command into the Input window.

Figure 1.5a *Commands that generate lists and reports*

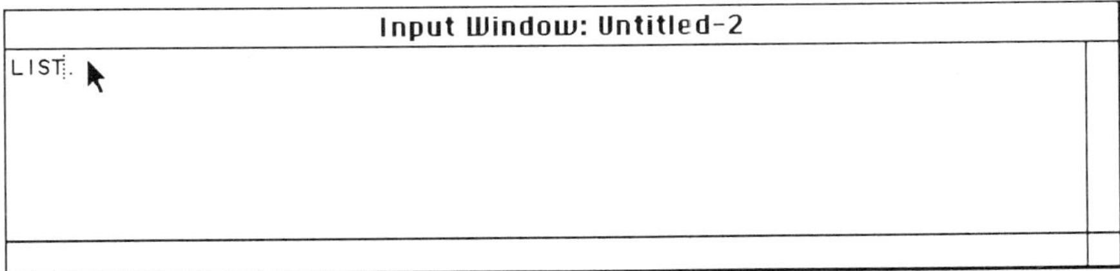

Since LIST is already selected in the list box, you have only to paste it.

❽ Click **Paste**. This pastes the LIST command into the Input window. Your Input window should resemble Figure 1.5b.

Figure 1.5b *The pasted LIST command*

Note: If you paste the wrong selection into your Input window, you can easily delete it. Click in the Input window and then drag across the text you want to delete. (If you select the wrong text, start dragging again.) Press the Delete key on your keyboard. This deletes the text. Then position the insertion point where you want the next selection to go, return to the Command Generator window, select the command you want, and paste it into the Input window. See Chapter R3 for more information on editing text in SPSS.

The LIST command should be in your Input window, followed by a period. The period is the *command terminator,* which indicates the end of the command. The period must be the last specification on every SPSS command; it signals that the command is complete.

You could run the LIST command with no subcommands to list all cases, but your goal is to list only the first 10 cases. To do this, you must paste the CASES subcommand into the Input window.

Be sure the insertion point is on the LIST command. The insertion point marks the position where additional selections from the Command Generator will be pasted. Since the Command Generator will not split a word, you can position the insertion point anywhere on the LIST command; SPSS will then assume you want to paste your next selection after LIST.

Now look at the Command Generator window. As you can see, when you clicked **Paste** to paste LIST into the Input window, SPSS automatically advanced to the next menu level.

❾ Click **/CASES**, and then click **Paste**.

1.6 Type in Specifications

The insertion point should still be just to the left of the period, which now follows the **CASES** subcommand. To specify the number of cases you want to list, you make the Input window active and type the number.

❿ Click in the Input window. This makes the Input window active and the insertion point starts blinking.

⓫ Type an equals sign and the number **10**. The text you type appears in the Input window.

You can always type specifications directly into the Input window as an alternative to pasting them from the list box.

1.7 RUN A COMMAND

Figure 1.7a shows the LIST command in the Input window. You are now ready to run the command.

Figure 1.7a *The LIST command in the Input window*

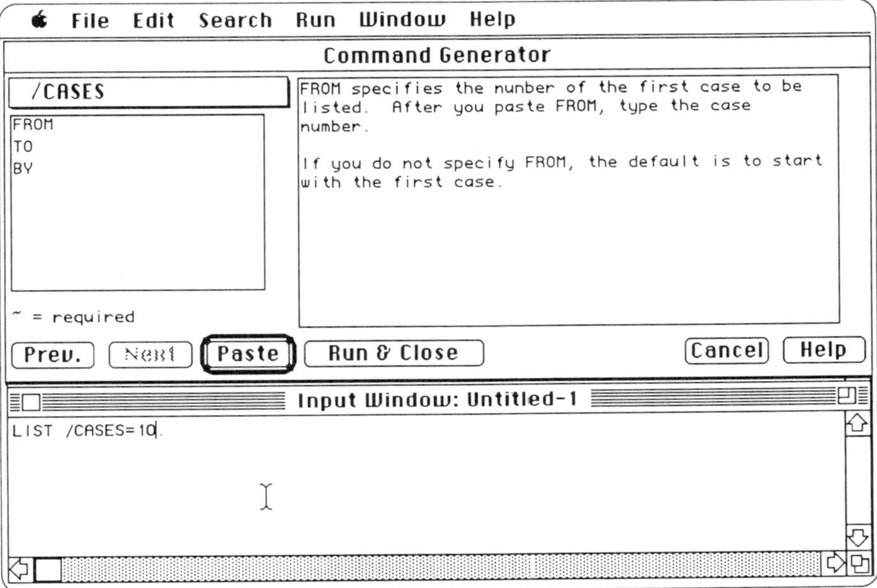

❶ Click in the Command Generator window to make it active.

❷ Click the **Run & Close** button. This runs the command that the insertion point is on in the Input window. The status box displays the name of the command that is running and a count of the number of cases processed so far. When the status box closes, the command is finished running, and the windows are arranged for comparing input and output.

Clicking **Run & Close** closes the Command Generator window and brings the Output window into view at the bottom of the screen. The Input window jumps to the top of the screen. Look at the output in your Output window. You should see the case listings shown in Figure 1.7b. (If you have set **Preferences** to turn off **Rearrange Windows**, the windows do not move.)

Figure 1.7b *Case listings generated by LIST*

```
 ⬢   File   Edit   Search   Run   Window   Help
                        Input Window: Untitled-1
LIST /CASES=10.
```

```
                              Output Window

  ID SALBEG SEX TIME    AGE SALNOW EDLEVEL    WORK JOBCAT MINORITY   SEXRACE

 628   8400  0  81    28.50  16080    16      .25    4       0        1.00
 630  24000  0  73    40.33  41400    16    12.50    5       0        1.00
 632  10200  0  83    31.08  21960    15     4.08    5       0        1.00
 633   8700  0  93    31.17  19200    16     1.83    4       0        1.00
 635  17400  0  83    41.92  28350    19    13.00    5       0        1.00
 637  12996  0  80    29.50  27250    18     2.42    4       0        1.00
 641   6900  0  79    28.00  16080    15     3.17    1       0        1.00
 649   5400  0  67    28.75  14100    15      .50    1       0        1.00
 650   5040  0  96    27.42  12420    15     1.17    1       0        1.00
 652   6300  0  77    52.92  12300    12    26.42    3       0        1.00
Number of cases read:   10     Number of cases listed:   10
```

1.8 DISPLAY LABELS IN THE VARIABLES WINDOW

When you see variable names like AGE and SEX in the output, you can probably guess what they represent. But what do variable names like SALBEG and SALNOW represent? To find out, you can open the Variables window.

❶ Choose **Variables Window** from the **Window** menu. This opens the Variables window, as shown in Figure 1.8a. The list box on the left displays the names of the variables in the file.

You may have noticed that the variable names all have eight characters or fewer. Names of variables in SPSS are limited to eight characters, which makes processing efficient. For ease in reading output, you can give each eight-character name a longer descriptive label. For more information on naming and labeling variables, see the *SPSS Base System User's Guide.*

Figure 1.8a *Variables window*

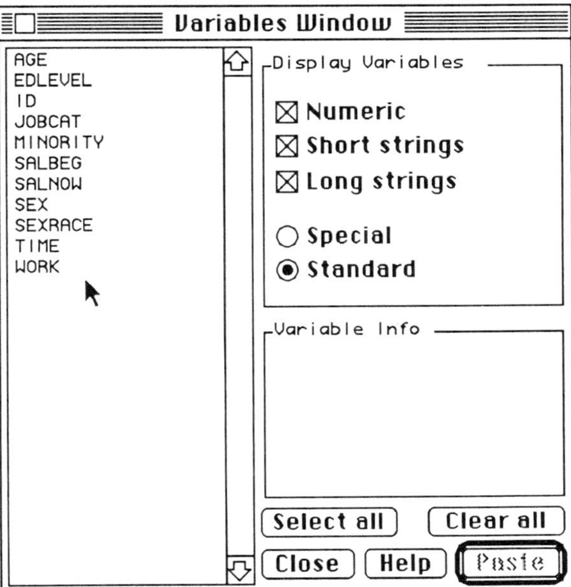

❷ Click variable **SALBEG** in the list box. The **Variable Info** box on the right displays the *variable label* (Beginning Salary) that was assigned to variable SALBEG. It also tells you that the type of variable is numeric.

❸ Press the Down Arrow key and position the highlight over **SALNOW** in the list box. The **Variable Info** box displays the label and variable type for SALNOW. Because variable labels in SPSS can be quite long, the **Variable Info** box displays only one label at a time.

Take a moment to look at the variable labels for JOBCAT, MINORITY, and SEX. Also look at any other labels you are curious about. When you have finished looking at variable labels,

❹ Click the close box or the **Cancel** button. This closes the Variables window.

The next section shows you how to paste variable names from the Variables window into the Input window.

1.9 PERFORM AN ANALYSIS

A good way to start any analysis is to obtain descriptive statistics for the variables. This gives you some idea of the values that occur in the data. For example, you can get frequency tables for the employment category, minority classification, and sex of employees.

❶ Choose **Command Generator** from the **Window** menu. It appears as you left it. The Input window is again below the Command Generator window.

❷ Move the pointer to the menu title **/CASES** and press the mouse button. A pull-down list of menus appears.

❸ Drag to **analyze data** and release the mouse button.

Figure 1.9a shows how the Command Generator window should appear. The option **lists and reports** is selected.

Figure 1.9a *Command Generator window*

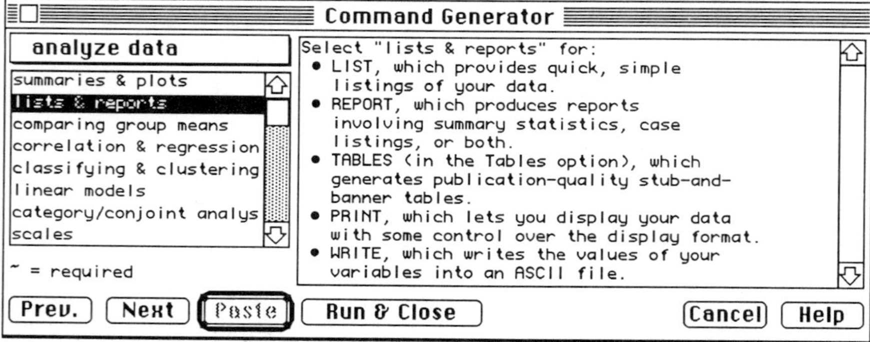

❹ Click **summaries and plots**. You should see **FREQUENCIES** among the commands described in the description window.

❺ Click **Next**.

❻ Click **FREQUENCIES** and then click **Next**. This puts FREQUENCIES in a holding area while you explore the subcommands.

Note: As an alternative you could paste the command at this time. But by using **Next** instead of **Paste**, you are free to back up and make changes later on without having to delete commands or subcommands that are already pasted into the Input window.

Now look in the Command Generator window. The menu in the list box shows the subcommands that are available for FREQUENCIES. The first subcommand, **VARIABLES**, is preceded by a tilde ($\sim$), which tells you the VARIABLES subcommand is required on the FREQUENCIES command. The slash identifies VARIABLES as a subcommand in SPSS.

❼ Click **Paste**. The FREQUENCIES command with the /VARIABLES subcommand is pasted on the line following the LIST command. SPSS automatically opens the Variables window.

The last variable name you selected earlier is still selected. Since you did not paste a variable name into the Input window, it is still highlighted. To select a variable name, click it. To undo a selection, select another variable or click the **Clear all** button. To select more than one variable name, press and hold the Command key while you click the names.

❽ Select **JOBCAT** and then hold down the Command key while you click **MINORITY** and **SEX**. (First undo any other selections you might have made earlier by clicking **JOBCAT**.) Your Variables window should resemble Figure 1.9b.

Figure 1.9b *Variables selected in the Variables window*

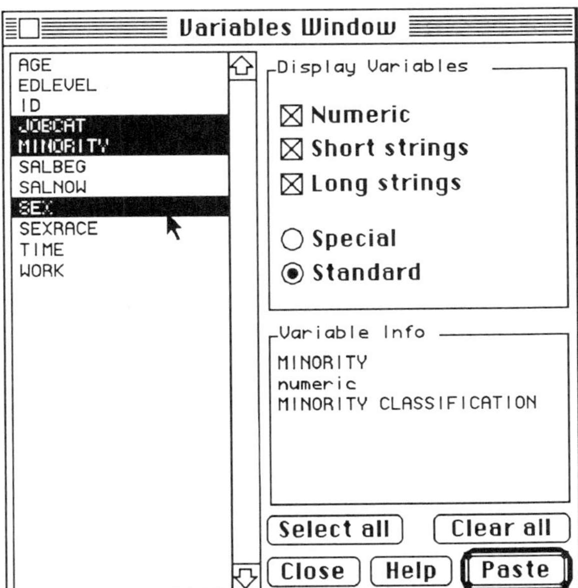

❾ Click **Paste**. This pastes the selected variable names into the Input window and closes the Variables window.

❿ Click **Barchart** and then click **Paste**. You are now ready to run the FREQUENCIES command.

⓫ Click the **Run & Close** in the Command Generator window. SPSS runs the command that the insertion point is on in the Input window.

1.10 VIEW THE OUTPUT

After the status dialog box closes, scroll through the Output window and view the frequency tables. Notice that the variable label is listed at the top of each frequency table and the value labels are listed at the left. Information on interpreting output is in the *SPSS Base System User's Guide.*

1.11 PRACTICE

If you would like to practice entering and running commands before ending the session, perform the following analyses:

DESCRIPTIVES Command. Compute the average age, education level, beginning salary, and current salary for each employee by entering and running the command:

```
DESCRIPTIVES /VARIABLES AGE EDLEVEL SALBEG SALNOW.
```

MEANS Command. Determine whether average beginning salaries differ by sex by entering and running the command:

```
MEANS /TABLES SALBEG BY SEX.
```

On the TABLES subcommand, specify SALBEG as the summary variable (choose **summary variable** from the menu and then paste variable **SALBEG** from the Variables window). Paste keyword **BY** into the Input window, and then specify SEX as the group variable (choose **group variable** from the menu and then paste variable **SEX** from the Variables window).

PLOT Command. Plot the relationship between beginning salary and current salary by entering and running the command:

```
PLOT /PLOT SALBEG WITH SALNOW.
```

When you paste the **PLOT** command into the Input window, available subcommands are displayed on the menu in the list box. The subcommand you want (the PLOT subcommand) is at the bottom of the list and not visible in the list box. Use the scroll bar in the list box to scroll to the bottom, and then select and paste **/PLOT**.

On the PLOT subcommand, specify SALBEG for the vertical axis (choose **vertical axis** from the menu and then paste variable **SALBEG** in the Variables window). Paste keyword **WITH** into the Input window and then specify SALNOW for the horizontal axis (choose **horizontal axis** from the menu and then paste variable **SALNOW** from the Variables window).

1.12 END AN SPSS SESSION

To end an SPSS session,

❶ Choose **Quit** from the **File** menu.

1.13 Save the Input Window as a Command File

After you choose **Quit**, a dialog box (shown in Figure 1.13a) asks whether you
want to save changes in the Input window. By saving them, you create an SPSS
command file, which is simply a file containing SPSS commands. You can open
and use command files in other SPSS sessions (Chapter 2 shows you how).

Figure 1.13a *Saving commands from the Input window*

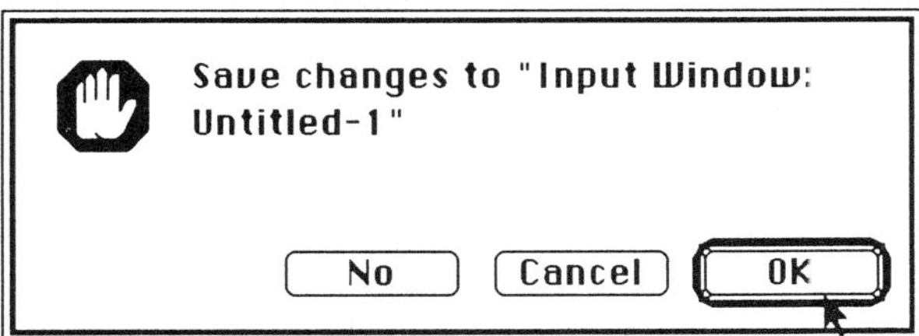

❶ Click **OK**. A directory dialog box appears. The current filename **Untitled-1** is in
the text box, **Save window Untitled-1 as**. Any text you type will replace the
highlighted text.

❷ Type **Bank.Commands** and click **Save**. This saves the commands in the Input
window into a command file named Bank.Commands. Bank.Commands is a
good filename to use because it associates the new command file with the SPSS
system file Bank.SPSS-Sys.

❸ After you click **Save**, another dialog box queries whether you want to save
changes in the Output window. Click **No**.

Of course, if you want to save the output from your session, you can click **OK**.
If you save the output from the Output window, you create an SPSS *listing file.*
A listing file is a text file that you can read into other applications. SPSS
automatically marks the file as a TEXT file. A good name for the file would be
Bank.Listing.

1.14 SUMMARY

- To start an SPSS session on the Mactintosh, double-click the **SPSS** icon.
- Within SPSS, you use the Input window to enter and run commands. SPSS uses the Output window to display output and the status dialog box to report on session status.
- To get an SPSS system file, you choose **Get SPSS System File** from the **File** menu, which opens a directory dialog box. Click the file you want, and then click **Get** to open the file.
- To use the SPSS Command Generator, choose **Command Generator Window** from the **Window** menu. The Command Generator lets you select commands and paste them into the Input window.
- You can type commands directly into the Input window.
- To delete entries from the Input window, use the mouse to select the text you do not want, and then press the Delete key on your keyboard.
- To type over text in the Input window, use the mouse to select the text you do not want, and then start typing the new text.
- To run a command, position the insertion point on that command in the Input window, and then click the **Run & Close** button in the Command Generator window.
- To see what variables are in the file, or to paste variable names into the Input window, you use the Variables window. To open the Variables window, choose **Variables Window** from the **Window** menu.
- To end an SPSS session, choose **Quit** from the **File** menu.
- Saving the commands in the Input window creates an SPSS command file (marked internally as type TEXT).
- Saving the output in the Output window creates an SPSS listing file (marked internally as type TEXT).

Chapter 2

Using SPSS Command Files

In Chapter 1 you used the SPSS Command Generator window to enter commands into the Input window. In this chapter, you will learn how to enter new commands into SPSS by another method— typing them directly into the Input window. You will see how to

- Open an SPSS command file.
- Run the commands in the file.
- Add new commands to the file.
- Save the revised command file.
- Run commands from a different file.

2.1 OPEN AN SPSS COMMAND FILE

To begin this tutorial you will open the command file Value.Commands, which you received with SPSS for the Macintosh. The file Value.Commands contains commands that define the data in the file Value.Data, which you also received.

❶ Begin an SPSS session (see Chapter 1 if you need more instructions).

❷ Choose **Open** from the **File** menu. This indicates you want to open an existing text file. A directory dialog box appears, as shown in Figure 2.1a.

❸ Click **Value** and then click **Open** (or double-click **Value**). The box lists the contents of the Value folder, including the command file Value.Commands. Several other SPSS command and data files are listed as well, including Value.Data.

Note: By default, SPSS puts an internal signature (type TEXT) on files it saves. When the Input window is active and you choose **Open**, only files with type TEXT are included in the list of files.

Figure 2.1a *Directory dialog box*

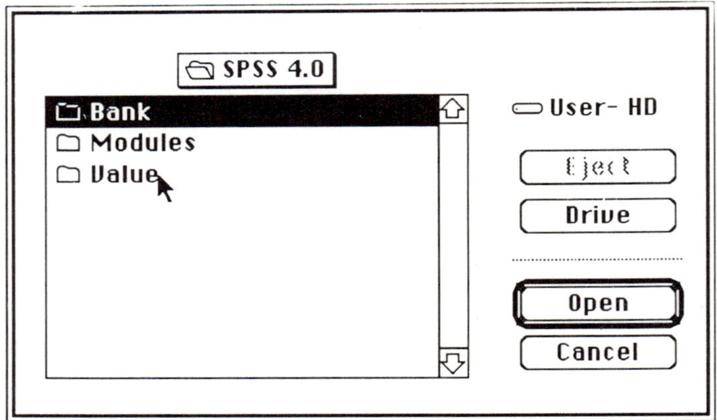

❹ Move the pointer to the list of files and click **Value.Commands.** This selects the file Value.Commands.

❺ Click **Open** (or double-click **Value.Commands**). This opens the file Value.Commands, as indicated on the Input window title bar.

❻ The file Value.Commands contains more command lines than can be displayed in the top half of your screen. To see all the commands in the Input window, click the zoom box in the top right corner of the window. This zooms the Input window. Though not visible, the Output window is open. Your screen should resemble Figure 2.1b.

Figure 2.1b *Commands from file Value.Commands*

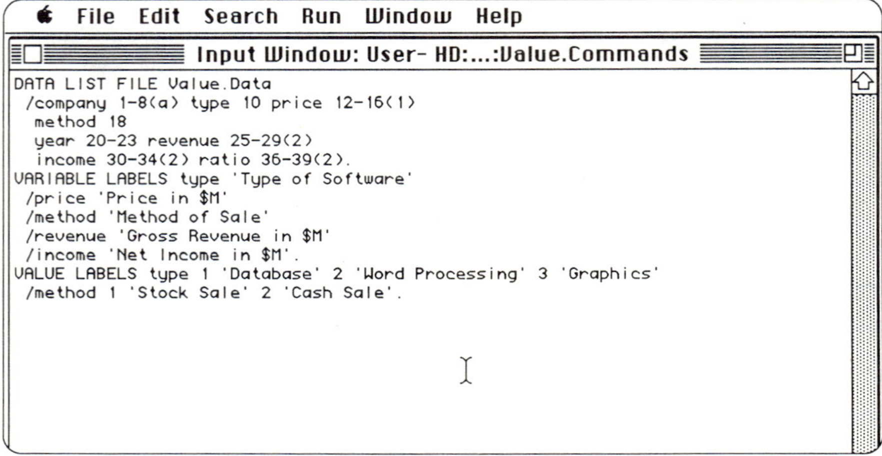

The commands in Value.Commands describe the data in the raw data file Value.Data, which contains information on 18 software companies that were sold between 1983 and 1987. The following information is available for each company:

- The name of the company.
- The selling price (in millions of dollars).
- The method of purchase (cash or stock).
- The year of sale.
- The company's revenue in the last year prior to sale (in millions of dollars).
- The company's income in the last year prior to sale (in millions of dollars).
- The ratio between each company's selling price and revenue.

2.2 MODIFY AND RUN COMMANDS

Opening an SPSS command file does not run the commands within the file. It simply brings those commands into the Input window. Once the commands are in the Input Window, you can run them. You can also add new commands or modify the existing commands.

2.3 Set the Directory

The FILE subcommand on the DATA LIST command in Value.Commands specifies a filename without a pathname (Value.Data). Thus, before you can run these commands, you need to set the directory where SPSS is to look. Otherwise SPSS will look in the application folder, SPSS 4.0, and display an error message.

❶ Choose **Set Directory** from the **File** menu. The directory named above the list box should be **Value.** If it is not, go up or down the hierarchy of files until Value is the directory.

❷ Click the **Set This Directory** button.

2.4 Type a New Command

The commands in Value.Commands simply define the data in file Value.Data. To produce a listing of the data values, we could add a LIST command after the existing commands.

As you can see on your screen, the insertion point is in the top-left corner of the Input window. To insert the LIST command after the existing commands, you must move the insertion point to the end of the window.

❸ Use the mouse to move the insertion point to the end of the last command. Press Return to start a new line so you can type a new command.

❹ Type **list.** Be sure to type the period at the end of the command.

2.5 Run the Commands

By default, SPSS runs only the command containing the insertion point. To run multiple commands, you must first select the commands you want to run, and then instruct SPSS to run them:

❺ Choose **Select All** from the **Edit** menu. This selects all commands in the Input window.

❻ Choose **Run Selection** from the **Run** menu. This runs the commands that are selected in the Input window. To see which command is running at any given moment, look in the status dialog box. Note that each command is deselected from the Input window as it is executed.

❼ Click the Input window's zoom box. This restores the Input window to its previous size, which brings the Output window back into view.

Figure 2.5a shows the listed data (with the size of the Output window adjusted).

Figure 2.5a *Case listings from file Value.Data*

```
                                    Output Window
COMPANY    TYPE   PRICE METHOD YEAR REVENUE  INCOME RATIO

SUPER        2     90.0    2   1987   41.50    7.80  2.17
DATAONE      1    108.4    2   1983   70.12    7.31  1.55
ALPHA        1    110.7    1   1983   51.17    7.23  2.16
DISK         2     54.8    2   1987   89.16    4.81   .61
MEGABYTE     2     17.0    1   1986   38.10    3.20   .45
HARDCORE     2     26.0    2   1986   17.20    3.20  1.51
VALUE        3     43.4    2   1985   38.09    2.45  1.14
BINARY       1      9.3    2   1984   13.25    2.26   .70
GRAND        1     27.5    1   1987   29.52    1.73   .93
NODOUBT      3     35.8    1   1986   40.31    1.59   .89
TRUE         3     37.5    2   1984   20.76    1.44  1.81
PLUS         1     23.1    1   1985   34.90    1.07   .66
POWER        3     20.0    2   1986   16.56    1.03  1.21
STEPUP       2     12.0    1   1983   15.54     .60   .77
KNOWIT       1      2.4    2   1987   43.01     .46   .06
LINEIT       3     33.9    1   1987   15.39    -.12  2.20
EXPOSE       3      2.3    2   1983   12.76    -.87   .18
LYRIC        2      6.3    2   1984   38.25    -.46   .16
Number of cases read:    18      Number of cases listed:    18
```

2.6 Add More Commands

As you look at the case listings in the Output window, you can see that the values for PRICE, REVENUE, INCOME and RATIO are displayed as standard numbers. It would be better if PRICE, REVENUE, and INCOME were displayed as dollar amounts, and RATIO as a percentage. You can accomplish this by specifying output formats for each of these variables.

❶ Click the zoom box to maximize the size of the Input window. This makes it easier to work in the window.

To position FORMATS before LIST, you create a blank line before the LIST command and then type the FORMATS command.

❷ Place the insertion point after **'Cash Sale'.** and press Return.

❸ Type **compute percent=100*ratio.** This converts each ratio value to a percentage.

❹ Type **formats price(dollar6.1) /revenue income(dollar6.2) /percent(pct5.0).** (Be sure to type the period, as shown.) This command indicates that PRICE will be displayed with a dollar sign and one decimal position, REVENUE and INCOME will be displayed with a dollar sign and two decimal positions, and PERCENT will be displayed with a percent sign and no decimal positions.

❺ Click anywhere within the COMPUTE command.

❻ Choose **Select Current to End** from the **Edit** menu. Because the insertion point was in the COMPUTE command, this selects the COMPUTE, FORMATS, and LIST commands. Your Input window should resemble Figure 2.6a.

Figure 2.6a *Input window*

```
Input Window: User- HD:...:Value.Commands
DATA LIST FILE "Value.Data"
 /company 1-8(a) type 10 price 12-16(1)
   method 18
   year 20-23 revenue 25-29(2)
   income 30-34(2) ratio 36-39(2).
VARIABLE LABELS type 'Type of Software'
 /price 'Price in $M'
 /method 'Method of Sale'
 /revenue 'Gross Revenue in $M'
 /income 'Net Income in $M'.
VALUE LABELS type 1 'Database' 2 'Word Processing' 3 'Graphics'
 /method 1 'Stock Sale' 2 'Cash Sale'.
compute percent=100*ratio.
formats price(dollar6.1) /revenue income(dollar6.2) /percent(pct5.0).
list.
```

❼ Press the Enter key. This is an alternative way to run the commands in the selected block.

❽ After the commands have been executed, click the zoom box to restore the Input window to its previous size.

When the SPSS Processor is ready, your Output window should resemble Figure 2.6b. As you can see, PRICE, REVENUE, INCOME, and PERCENT are displayed with their new formats.

Figure 2.6b *Case listings with the new formats*

```
                          Output Window
COMPANY   TYPE   PRICE METHOD YEAR REVENUE INCOME RATIO PERCENT

SUPER      2     $90.0    2   1987  $41.50  $7.80  2.17   217%
DATAONE    1    $108.4    2   1983  $70.12  $7.31  1.55   155%
ALPHA      1    $110.7    1   1983  $51.17  $7.23  2.16   216%
DISK       2     $54.8    2   1987  $89.16  $4.81   .61    61%
MEGABYTE   2     $17.0    1   1986  $38.10  $3.20   .45    45%
HARDCORE   2     $26.0    2   1986  $17.20  $3.20  1.51   151%
VALUE      3     $43.4    2   1985  $38.09  $2.45  1.14   114%
BINARY     1      $9.3    2   1984  $13.25  $2.26   .70    70%
GRAND      1     $27.5    1   1987  $29.52  $1.73   .93    93%
NODOUBT    3     $35.8    1   1986  $40.31  $1.59   .89    89%
TRUE       3     $37.5    2   1984  $20.76  $1.44  1.81   181%
PLUS       1     $23.1    1   1985  $34.90  $1.07   .66    66%
POWER      3     $20.0    2   1986  $16.56  $1.03  1.21   121%
STEPUP     2     $12.0    1   1983  $15.54   $.60   .77    77%
KNOWIT     1      $2.4    2   1987  $43.01   $.46   .06     6%
LINEIT     3     $33.9    1   1987  $15.39  -$.12  2.20   220%
EXPOSE     3      $2.3    2   1983  $12.76  -$.87   .18    18%
LYRIC      2      $6.3    2   1984  $38.25  -$.46   .16    16%
Number of cases read:   18    Number of cases listed:   18
```

2.7 SAVE THE COMMAND FILE

You have added the LIST, COMPUTE, and FORMATS commands to the Input window, but that does not add them to the original command file Value.Commands. You can add these commands to Value.Commands by simply saving the commands in the Input window. You can also save the commands into a new file.

Assume you do not want to save the LIST command in the command file. You must therefore delete it from the Input window before you save the file.

❶ Click the zoom box to maximize the size of the Input window.

❷ Move the I-beam to the beginning of the **list** command in the Input window, drag to select the entire **list** command, and release the mouse button.

❸ Press the Delete key. This deletes the selected line.

❹ Choose **Save As** from the **File** menu. This opens a directory dialog box. The current document name is selected in the **Save window** text box.

❺ Click between Value and the period, and type **Format** in the **Save window** text box. The name of the new file is now **ValueFormat.Commands.**

❻ Click **Save.** This saves commands in the Input window into the new file ValueFormat.Commands. The Input window title bar indicates that ValueFormat.Commands is now the open file. The original file Value.Commands is unchanged.

As you can see, saving the commands does not close the Input window. Thus, you can continue working.

Note: If you mistakenly choose **Save** instead of **Save As** from the **File** menu, commands in the Input window replace the commands in file Value.Commands. No harm is done in this tutorial, but in your own work you should be careful not to choose **Save** unless you want to replace the contents of the original file you opened.

2.8 RUNNING COMMANDS FROM A DIFFERENT COMMAND FILE

With SPSS for the Macintosh you received a file called ValueReport.Commands. This SPSS command file contains a REPORT command for obtaining a report on the data in the file Value.Data. You can open this file in another Input window and then run the commands.

❶ Choose **Open** from the **File** menu. A dialog box appears, as shown in Figure 2.8a.

Figure 2.8a *Open dialog box*

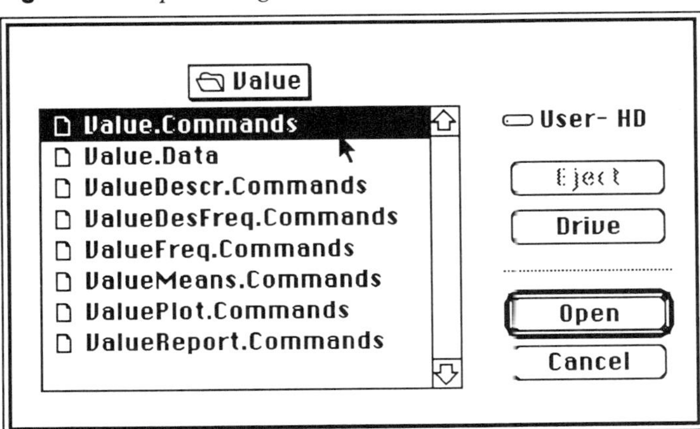

❷ Click the name **ValueReport.Commands** to select it.

❸ Click **Open**. As shown in Figure 2.8b, this opens a new Input window containing commands from the selected file. In this instance, the SORT CASES and REPORT commands from the command file ValueReport.Commands appear.

❹ Choose **Select All** from the **Edit** menu.

❺ Choose **Run Selection** from the **Run** menu. This runs the SPSS commands.

Figure 2.8b *Commands in file ValueReportCommands*

```
Input Window: User- HD:...:ValueReport.Commands
SORT CASES BY TYPE.
REPORT  /FORMAT AUTOMATIC LIST
 /VARIABLES=company price revenue income ratio
 /BREAK=type
 /SUMMARY=MEAN .
```

Note: These commands run because you already ran the DATA LIST command to define an active SPSS system file. They would generate errors (listed in the Output window) if you had not already defined an active system file, or if they used variables that were not on the current active system file.

On your own, you can study the report in the Output window. To do so, click in the Output window to make it active and use the scroll bar to scroll through the output.

You can end the session now, or go on to the practice section. To end the session, choose **Quit** from the **File** menu. Refer to Chapter 1 for details.

2.9 PRACTICE

If you have not ended the session you started in this chapter, you can practice opening and inserting command files using the files listed below (you received these files with SPSS for the Macintosh). If you want to practice with these files some other time, you must first open the file ValueFormat.Commands and then define an active SPSS system file by selecting and running all the commands in the file.

Once you have defined an active system file, you can run the commands in each of the files named below by making the Input window active and choosing **Open** from the **File** menu. Then select the commands and run them.

ValueFreq.Commands.   The FREQUENCIES command in this command file obtains frequency tables for type of software company, method of sale, and year of sale.

ValueDescr.Commands.   The DESCRIPTIVES command in this command file obtains the mean, standard deviation, minimum, maximum, and valid number of cases for selling price, revenue, income, and price-to-revenue ratio.

ValueMeans.Commands.   The MEANS command in this command file tests whether the average selling price differed for the types of companies.

ValuePlot.Commands.   The PLOT command in this command file plots the relationship between selling price and income for all eighteen companies.

2.10   SUMMARY

- To work with SPSS command files, use the menu commands available on the **File** menu.
- Opening an SPSS command file does not run the commands within the file. It simply brings those commands into the Input window.
- You can maximize the Input window by clicking the zoom box for the window. If you run any commands while the window is maximized, you will have to click the zoom box again to restore the window to its previous size before you can see any SPSS output.
- By default, SPSS runs only the command containing the insertion point. To run multiple commands, first select the commands you want to run and then instruct SPSS to run them.
- To select all commands in the Input window, choose **Select All** from the **Edit** menu (the Input window must be active).
- To select a block of SPSS commands from the insertion point to the end of the Input window, position the insertion point anywhere within the first command you want in the block. Then choose **Select Current to End** from the **Edit** menu.
- To run a selected (highlighted) block of commands, choose **Run Selection** from the **Run** menu.
- At any time during an SPSS session you can save the commands in the Input window into a command file, which you can reopen at any time. Saving the commands in the Input window does not close the Input window.
- To delete commands from the Input window, select the commands you want to delete and then press the Delete key.

Chapter R1

SPSS Menus and Windows

This chapter describes the menus and windows used in SPSS for the Macintosh. The menus in this chapter are in the order they appear on the menu bar. Special windows are described under the **Windows** menu (see Section R1.35).

In general:

- You can get help at any time. Either choose **Help** from the **Help** menu or press Command-H to request information about the current window or dialog box.

- You can cancel a selection from any window or box that contains a **Cancel** button.

- You can use keyboard equivalents as shortcuts for many menu options. Keyboard equivalents are identified on the menus to the right of each option.

- Menu options and buttons are disabled and dimmed if they have no current function.

- An ellipsis (...) after a menu option indicates the option opens a window or dialog box.

- A right arrowhead (>) after a menu option indicates the option opens a submenu.

R1.1 APPLE MENU

From the **Apple** menu you can obtain information about the current application, open desk accessories, and switch among applications when Multifinder is on. The menu shown in Figure R1.1a shows a typical list of desk accessories. Since only the first command pertains specifically to SPSS, it is the only one described here.

Figure R1.1a *Apple menu*

R1.2 About SPSS

About SPSS displays a message box with the release number and date, icon, and copyright notice for SPSS for the Macintosh. This lets you know which release of SPSS for the Macintosh you are using. Click anywhere in the box to return to the SPSS program.

R1.3 FILE MENU

The commands on the **File** menu let you create new files, work with existing files, print windows, set the directory, or quit SPSS.

- The **Open** or **New** command opens an Input window. You can have up to ten Input windows open at once.
- To edit any saved TEXT file, such as a command or listing file, open an Input window.
- **Get SPSS System File, Save SPSS System File, Get Data File,** and **Save Data File** always pertain to data files.

Untitled Documents.   When you begin a session, SPSS opens an untitled Input window and an untitled Output window. Each untitled window is essentially a temporary, untitled document, and the document is not saved on disk unless you save it. Once you save the document, the name you assign to it is shown in the window's title bar, along with the disk name.

File Commands.   Most commands in the **File** menu apply to command files when the Input window is active, and output files when the Output window is active. However, **Open** or **New** always opens an Input window, and **Close** always closes the *active* Input window.

Data Files.   In many cases, you can bring data directly into SPSS by simply choosing one of the **Get** commands from the **File** menu. For more information on how to get data into SPSS using specific types of files, see Chapter R2.

Figure R1.3a *File menu*

```
 File
▶New                 ⌘N
  Open...             ⌘O
  Close               ⌘W
  Save                ⌘S
  Save As...
  Append Window...
 .............................
  Get SPSS System File...
  Save SPSS System File...
 .............................
  Get Data File         ▶
  Save Data File        ▶
 .............................
  Page Setup...
  Print Window...
 .............................
  Set Directory...
 .............................
  Quit                 ⌘Q
```

R1.4 New

New opens a new untitled Input window. Use it to enter SPSS commands.

R1.5 Open

Open opens a new Input window and loads an existing file into it. Use it to:

- Display the contents of an existing file.
- Edit an existing file of SPSS commands.
- Edit a saved output file.

When you choose **Open,** a directory dialog box appears (see Chapter R2 or your Macintosh *User's Guide* for more information). When the file is selected, click the **Open** button. If you change your mind, you can click the **Cancel** button, which cancels the request to open a file and returns the insertion point to the active window.

Note: Creating a new Input window does *not* clear or otherwise affect the active SPSS system file if one is open. Thus, if the commands in the file you open do not pertain to the current active system file, you must define a new active file to continue working. See the *SPSS Base System User's Guide* for a discussion of the active system file.

R1.6 Close

Close closes the active Input window. (You cannot close the Output window.) A dialog box asks whether you want to save any changes made in the window. **OK** replaces the contents of the file that has the name in the title bar and closes the window. **No** closes the window without saving changes made since the last **Save** or **Save As.**

Clicking the close box of the Input window is equivalent to choosing **Close** from the **File** menu.

R1.7 Save

Save saves the contents of the active window, or a selected area from the active window, into the file named in the title bar. Use it to save contents of the active window in their current state and continue working with the same contents. If the active window is untitled, **Save** is dimmed; use **Save As** instead.

Caution: If the original contents of the active window came from an existing file (the file is identified in the title bar), the current contents from the active window replace contents from the original file. Do not use **Save** unless you want to replace the contents of the original file. To preserve the contents of the original file, use **Save As** instead.

R1.8 Save As

Save As saves the contents of the active window into a new file. Use it when you opened and modified the contents of an existing file and want to save the modified file into a new file, without changing the contents of the original file. You can then continue working with the same contents. To name the new file, you use a directory dialog box (see Chapter R2).

R1.9 Append Window or Append Selection

Append copies the contents of the active window, or a selected area in the active window, to the end of a file and lets you continue working with the same window.

- **Append Selection** appears on the menu when text is selected. It copies the contents of the selected area in the active window to the end of the receiving file.
- **Append Window** appears on the menu when text is not selected. It copies the complete contents of the window to the end of the receiving file.

To start the action, click the **Append** button. To specify the receiving file, use the directory dialog box (see Chapter R2).

R1.10 Get SPSS System File

Get SPSS System File retrieves an SPSS system file, which is a special type of data file created by SPSS. The dialog box displays only files marked internally with the SPSS system file type.

R1.11 Save SPSS System File

Save SPSS System File saves an SPSS system file. SPSS for the Macintosh marks the file internally as an SPSS system file. You can give it any name up to

31 characters. The SPSS system files you received with the program include .SPSS-Sys in the name so that you will be able to recognize this type of file when you see it on a list of files.

R1.12 Get Data File

Get Data File opens a submenu from which you choose the type of file to get (see Figure R1.12a). Note that this option cannot be used to read raw data files. To read a raw data file, you must enter a command that defines the raw data file (such as a DATA LIST command) into the Input window and then run that command.

Figure R1.12a *Get Data submenu*

Each of the following options opens a dialog box for selecting the data file:

- **Portable** gets an SPSS portable file. Portable files are SPSS system files that can be read and written by SPSS on different operating systems (with the IMPORT and EXPORT commands). The dialog box displays all files.
- **SYLK** gets a Multiplan spreadsheet or an Excel file saved in SYLK format (or any other SYLK file). The dialog box displays only files saved in SYLK format.
- **Tab Delimited** gets a tab-delimited file. You can use these files in other applications such as spreadsheets or databases. The dialog box displays files with type TEXT.

The following defaults are in effect for SYLK files:

- By default, SPSS gets the entire file. To indicate a range from the file, enter the range in the **Range** text box, as in **r1c1:r14c11.**
- By default, SPSS does not read variable names from the first row of the range. To read the variable names, click the check box to the left of **Read Variable Names.**

For more information on reading a SYLK file, see the GET TRANSLATE command in the *SPSS Reference Guide.*

R1.13 Save Data File

Save Data File opens a submenu from which you indicate the type of file to save (see Figure R1.13a).

Figure R1.13a *Save Data submenu*

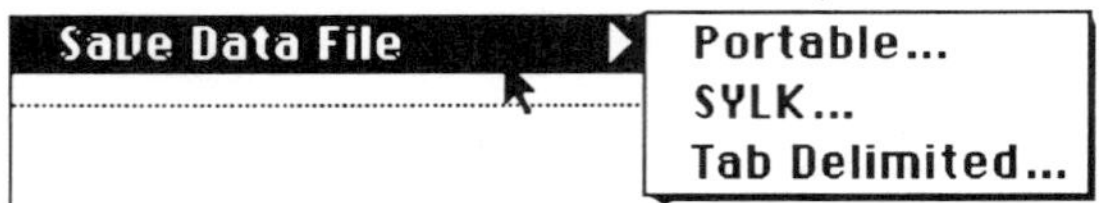

Each of the following options opens a dialog box for naming the data file (see Chapter R2):

- **Portable** saves an SPSS portable file. You can use a portable file in SPSS on other operating systems, such as DOS.
- **SYLK** saves a spreadsheet file in SYLK format. By default, SPSS does not save variable names from the first row of the range. To save the variable names, click **Save variable names** to put an **X** in the check box. A SYLK file can be used in Multiplan or Excel.
- **Tab Delimited** saves a file in tab-delimited format. These files can be read by many spreadsheet or database applications.

Caution: If you open a non-SPSS file, such as a spreadsheet file, you should save the file under a new name instead of its original name. SPSS discards information such as formulas and range names when it saves the file, and it will overwrite the previous spreadsheet file if you save it under the old name.

R1.14 Page Setup

Page Setup opens a standard Macintosh dialog box that defines print options, such as paper size, reduction, and orientation (portrait or landscape). The features depend on your printer. If you click **Page Setup** when the Output window is active and choose a page size, the program will also generate the SPSS commands that set the width and length of subsequent output to conform to the page size chosen.

R1.15 Print Window

Print Window prints the contents of the active window. A standard Macintosh print dialog box appears, depending on which type of printer you have selected in the Chooser. Unless you have run a SET HEADERS OFF command, lines appear in your **Output** window indicating page breaks. These lines are not printed;

header information, including date, SPSS version (or a title specified on the
SPSS TITLE command), and page number, is printed at the top of each page.
See Appendix B for more information.

- **Cancel** cancels the print request.

R1.16 Print Selection

Print Selection prints only the text you have selected. You can select text by
dragging or by choosing one of the options from the **Edit** menu. When you
choose **Print Selection,** a standard Macintosh print dialog box appears,
depending on which type of printer you have selected in the Chooser. Leave
the **Pages** radio button selection on **All.** See Appendix B for more information.

- **Cancel** cancels the print request.

R1.17 Set Directory

Set Directory accesses a dialog box that lets you select the directory for running
SPSS commands that contain filenames without pathnames. (A pathname
gives the disk drive and folders necessary to find the file.) SPSS will use the
directory selected in the **Set Directory** dialog box to determine the pathname
(see Figure R1.17a). If you do not set the directory, SPSS will look in the SPSS
application folder for files, regardless of the current directory for *opening* files.
If the file is not there, an error message appears in the Output window. If you
use a complete pathname within apostrophes on an SPSS command, SPSS will
follow the pathname, not the set directory. For more information on how to
identify files and specify pathnames, see Chapter R2.

Figure R1.17a *Set Directory dialog box*

Select This Directory

SPSS 4.0   User- HD

Bank
Modules
Value

Eject

Drive

Open

Directory

Cancel

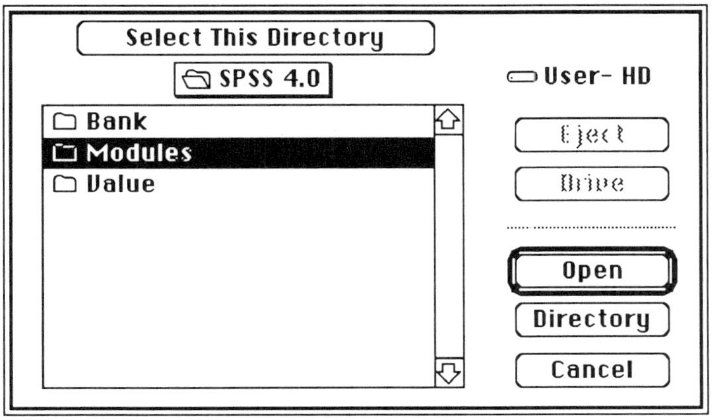

- The **Select This Directory** button at the top selects the directory named above the list of folders. In Figure R1.17a, if you click the **Select This Directory** button, the directory will be SPSS 4.0.
- The **Directory** button selects the directory highlighted in the list of folders. In Figure R1.17a, if you click the **Directory** button, the directory **Modules** is selected.
- When you click either the **Select This Directory** or **Directory** button, a SET DIRECTORY command is run and appears in the Output window.
- If you click the **Open** button, the Modules folder is opened and you can proceed from there with selecting a directory.

If you want to know what directory you are in, you can run a SHOW DIRECTORY command and look in the Output window for the results. Then if you type in a command such as

```
DATA LIST FILE=EMPLOYEES ...
```

SPSS will look for the EMPLOYEES file in the directory indicated.

R1.18 Quit

Quit exits from SPSS. If any Input window or the Output window contains information that has not been saved, a dialog box queries whether you want to save the changes. If other windows are open, a dialog box asks about saving each window.

- **OK** opens a dialog box so you can name the file.
- **No** closes the window.
- **Cancel** cancels the Quit request and returns you to the SPSS session.

R1.19 EDIT MENU

The commands in the **Edit** menu let you edit the contents of the active window and select areas in the active window. (This chapter describes only the **Edit** *menu* commands. See Chapter R3 for information on available editing keys and functions.)

The **Edit** menu usually works the same whether the Input or Output window is active. The only exception is in selecting areas:

- When the Input window is active, **Edit** lets you select an entire command, even if some lines of that command are above the line containing the insertion point.
- When the Output window is active, **Edit** cannot select lines that are above the insertion point line.

Figure R1.19a *Edit menu for the Input window*

```
 Edit
Can't Undo          ⌘Z
.........................
Cut                 ⌘X
Copy                ⌘C
Paste               ⌘U
Clear
Copy Table
.........................
Round...
.........................
Select Command     ⌘E
Select Current to End
Select All         ⌘A
.........................
Preferences...
```

Figure R1.19b *Edit menu for the Output window*

```
 Edit
Can't Undo          ⌘Z
.........................
Cut                 ⌘X
Copy                ⌘C
Paste               ⌘U
Clear
Copy Table
.........................
Round...
.........................
Select Command     ⌘E
Select Current to End
Select All         ⌘A
.........................
Preferences...
```

R1.20 Undo

Undo undoes the last editing operation. For example, if you type something into an active window, **Undo** deletes what you just typed into that window. Depending upon your most recent editing action, the text of the menu option changes to reflect what can be undone. For example:

- **Undo Typing** deletes the text most recently typed. The remaining text reverts to its previous condition.
- **Undo Paste** deletes pasted text. The text reverts to its condition before the paste operation.
- **Undo Cut** pastes the cut text back into the file. The text remains on the Clipboard.

R1.21 Redo

Redo sometimes appears in place of **Undo. Redo** reverses the previous **Undo.**

R1.22 Cut

Cut removes the contents of a selected area from the active window and stores them on the Clipboard, from which you can retrieve them with **Paste.** Text in the active window shifts to fill the space left by the cut text. Use **Cut** to move window contents from one place to another.

The cut information remains on the Clipboard until replaced by another **Cut** or **Copy.** You can see the contents of the Clipboard by choosing **Clipboard Window** from the **Window menu.**

R1.23 Copy

Copy copies the contents of a selected area from the active window and stores them on the Clipboard, from which you can retrieve them with **Paste.** Use **Copy** to copy window contents from one place to another.

The copied information remains on the Clipboard until replaced by another **Cut** or **Copy.** The active window is unaffected.

R1.24 Paste

Paste copies the contents of the Clipboard (stored by **Cut** or **Copy** or another software program) into the active window, beginning at the insertion point.

Contents of the clipboard are not affected. Thus, you can paste a copy of the same contents again to another area.

You can paste contents into the Input window, the Output window, or into a text box within a dialog box or pop-up window. For example, you can copy a phrase into the **Search string** text box on the Glossary window.

- To paste into a text box, you must use the keyboard equivalent Command-V, because you cannot use the menus when a pop-up window or dialog box is open.

- Contents that you paste do not cause lines to wrap. The maximum length for a single line is 255 columns; SPSS will not paste contents that will cause a line to exceed 255 columns.

- If you don't remember what is on the Clipboard, you can open the Clipboard window from the **Windows** menu.

R1.25 Clear

Clear removes the contents of a selected area from the active window without storing them on the clipboard. Use **Clear** to erase information from the active window. The Clear and Delete keys on your keyboard accomplish the same thing.

R1.26 Copy Table

Copy Table saves selected columns on the Clipboard in tab-delimited format (with tabs between the columns). You can use this function to

- Transfer data to a spreadsheet or graph-making application (for example, Excel or Cricket Graph). The entries will be inserted in the cells.
- Transfer results into a word processing application. For example, you can copy a table of frequencies from SPSS output into Microsoft Word and then use the **Insert Table** command of Microsoft Word to adjust the table.

R1.27 Round

Round rounds off or truncates numbers within a selected area in the active window. When you click **Round,** a dialog box pops up (Figure R1.27a).

❶ Enter the number of decimal positions. The default is 0 decimal positions.

❷ Click **Round** or **Truncate.**

The **Round** radio button rounds all numbers within the selection to the specified number of decimal positions, while **Truncate** truncates them. The option you select remains in effect the next time you select **Round** from the **Edit** menu, unless you change it.

Figure R1.27a *Round Numbers dialog box*

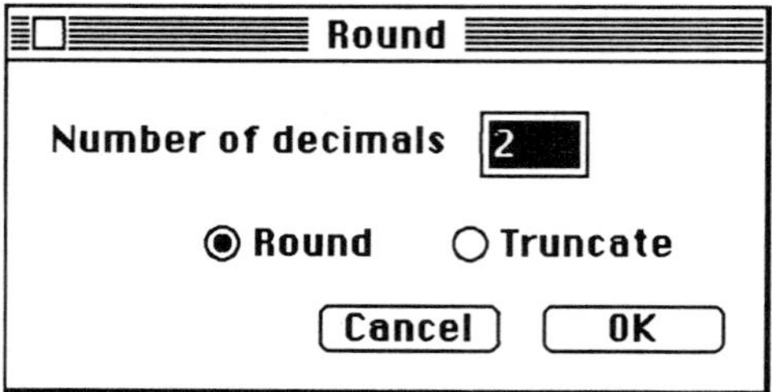

R1.28 Select Commands (in the Input Window)

The **Edit** menu contains three commands for selecting SPSS commands already entered in the active Input window:

- **Select Command** selects the complete command containing the insertion point, even if some lines of the command are above the insertion point.
- **Select Current to End** selects multiple commands, beginning with the command that contains the insertion point and ending with the last command in the Input window.
- **Select All** selects all commands in the Input window.

R1.29 Select Lines (in the Output Window)

If the Output window is active, the **Edit** menu contains two commands for selecting lines:

- **Select Current to End** selects multiple lines, beginning with the line containing the insertion point and ending with the last line in the Output window.
- **Select All** selects all lines in the Output window.

R1.30 Preferences

Preferences opens a dialog box for you to customize your SPSS sessions (see Figure R1.30a).

Figure R1.30a *Preferences dialog box*

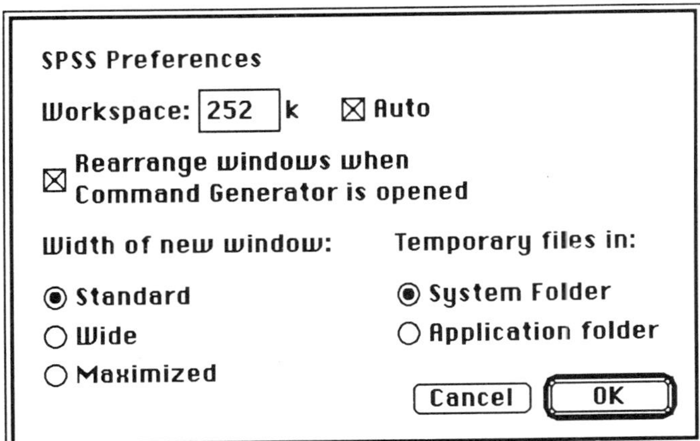

To implement a workspace or window-size change chosen from the **Preferences** dialog box, you must quit SPSS and begin a new session. The changes you make in this dialog box remain in subsequent sessions until you change them again.

- **Workspace** allows you to specify the number of kilobytes allotted to SPSS workspace. To override the default workspace allocation, type the number of kilobytes in the text box. **Auto** lets SPSS allocate the workspace. SPSS calculates the optimum, given the available memory. See Chapter R2 for more information on customizing the amount of workspace for your session.

- **Rearrange windows when Command Generator is opened.** SPSS opens with the Input window at the top of the screen and the Output window below it. When you open the Command Generator window, the Input window and the Output window switch places so that you can see the commands being generated. As an alternative, you can move the Command Generator window the first time you open it so you can see the Input window. This method works well with large display monitors. To prevent the Input and Output windows from moving when you open the Command Generator window, click the check box so that the **X** disappears and then click the box again.

- **Width of new window** offers three choices for the width of newly opened windows: **Standard** width accommodates approximately 80 characters of 9-point SPSSfont; **Wide** accommodates approximately 132 characters of 9-point SPSSfont; and **Maximized** indicates that each newly opened window will use the maximum width available on your monitor. If you have a small monitor and choose **Wide** or **Maximized**, SPSS ignores the preference and uses **Standard** width.

- **Temporary files in:** indicates the location of temporary files that SPSS creates during a session. Normally, temporary files are deleted at the end of a session, but in abnormal circumstances, such a file can remain on the disk. **System Folder** places the temporary files in the *Macintosh System folder*. **Application Folder** places the temporary files in the same folder that has the *SPSS application icon*.

Click the **OK** button when you are satisfied with your choices. **Cancel** closes the dialog box without making any changes.

R1.31 SEARCH MENU

The **Search** menu allows you to find specific text segments in a file. It works the same whether the Input or Output window is active.

Figure R1.31a *Search menu*

R1.32 Find

Find searches the active window until it finds the next occurrence of a string of characters and selects it. The search begins from the insertion point. To specify the string, you use a dialog box (Figure R1.32a).

Figure R1.32a *Find dialog box*

The first time you use the **Find** dialog box, the **Search string** text box is blank. Once you specify a search string, that string becomes the default for the next use. The steps for using this box are as follows:

❶ By default, SPSS ignores case (**a** is the same as **A**). For a case-sensitive search, click an **X** into the **Case sensitive** check box.

❷ Specify the search string in the **Search string** text box. Usually you will type the string. However, you can also use Command-V to paste a string that was stored on the Clipboard by a previous **Cut** or **Copy**.

❸ To start the search, click either **Find forward** or **Find backward**. This determines whether **Find** searches forward or backward from the insertion point. Initially, **Find forward** is the default; the search will be a forward search if you press Return instead of clicking a button.

R1.33 Search and Replace

Search and Replace searches the active window for the next occurrence of a character string and then replaces that string with another. The search begins from the insertion point. When you choose **Search and Replace** from the **Search** menu, the **Search and Replace** dialog box appears (Figure R1.33a).

Figure R1.33a *Search and Replace dialog box*

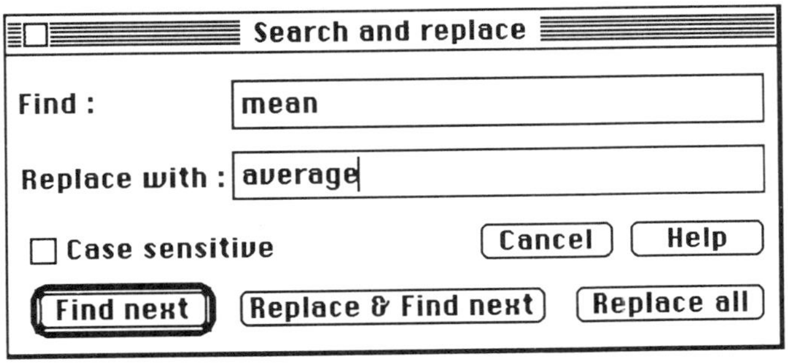

Search and replace

Find :   mean

Replace with :   average

☐ Case sensitive   Cancel   Help

Find next   Replace & Find next   Replace all

The first time you use the **Search and Replace** dialog box, the **Find** and **Replace with** text boxes are blank. Once you specify strings in these boxes, they become the defaults for the next use. You can type the strings into these text boxes, or press Command-V to retrieve a string that was stored on the Clipboard by a previous **Cut** or **Copy**.

❶ Specify the search string in the **Find** text box. *Do not* press Return. Use the mouse or the Tab key to move the insertion point to the next text box.

Note: Pressing Return is equivalent to clicking the active button. Since **Find next** is the active button in this instance, pressing Return finds the first occurrence of the string and then awaits your instructions. When you perform Step 4, you must remember that you have already found the first occurrence of the string; to replace, click the **Replace & Find next** button.

❷ Click or tab to the **Replace with** text box and specify a replacement string. If you leave this box blank, the string will be deleted.

❸ By default, SPSS ignores case (**a** is the same as **A**). For a case-sensitive search-and-replace operation, click an **X** into the **Case Sensitive** check box.

❹ To initiate the search, click **Find next**. You must click **Find next** before you can click **Replace & Find next**. The system finds the requested string, selects it in the active window, and waits for further instructions.

❺ To replace the string, click either **Replace & Find next** or **Replace all**. If you do not want to replace the string, click **Find next** again or click **Cancel.**

- **Replace & Find next** replaces the selected string, finds the next occurrence, and waits for further instructions. If you do not want to replace the next occurrence, click **Find next** again or **Cancel.**

- **Replace All** replaces all occurrences of the string. **Replace All** does not stop until it reaches the end of the active window. It replaces every occurrence of the string.

- **Cancel** cancels the search-and-replace operation.

R1.34 RUN MENU

The **Run** menu lets you run one or more selected commands. If you choose **Run Selection** from the **Run** menu, the system runs the command on which the insertion point currently appears (the insertion point can be just to the left of, or anywhere within, the command). If a set of commands is selected in the Input window, all selected commands are run sequentially, one after the other. **Run Selection** is available only when the Input window is active. Otherwise, it is dimmed.

Figure R1.34a *Run Selection*

As an alternative to choosing **Run Selection** from the menu, you can use the keyboard equivalent Command-R or press the Enter key.

R1.35 WINDOW MENU

The **Window** menu has several functions. It

- Provides access to the SPSS Command Generator window for entering commands into the Input window.
- Provides access to the Glossary window for looking up statistical and SPSS terms.
- Provides access to the Variables window for viewing variable names and labels and for pasting variable names into the Input window.
- Determines the arrangement of windows in SPSS, and whether the Input window or Output window is active.

Windows that are open are preceded by a diamond shape. The active window is indicated by a filled-in diamond.

Figure R1.35a *Window menu*

R1.36 Arrange All

Arrange All restores all SPSS windows to their default size and position. The default size can be changed by choosing **Preferences** from the **Edit** menu.

R1.37 Command Generator

Command Generator opens the Command Generator window, from which you can enter commands into the Input window by *pasting* menu selections. It also provides descriptions and examples for SPSS commands, subcommands, and keywords.

The Command Generator window (Figure R1.37a) can be opened, closed, and moved. It cannot be resized. If the Command Generator window is open, it obscures the Output window on small monitors.

Figure R1.37a *Command Generator window*

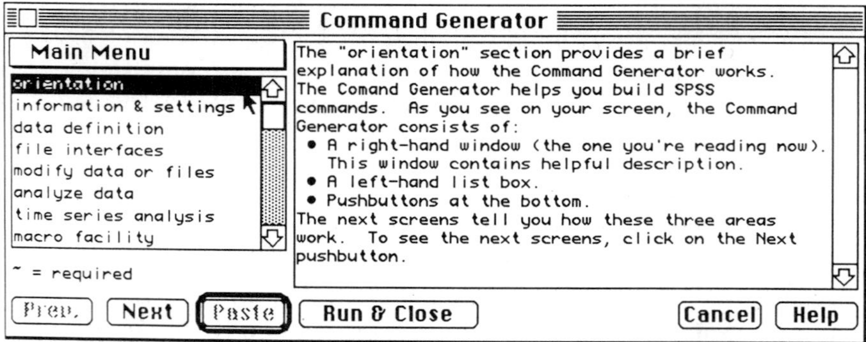

Detailed instructions for using the Command Generator window are in Chapter R2.

R1.38 Glossary Window

Glossary Window is used to obtain definitions for statistical and SPSS terms. If you request a definition for a term that is not in the glossary, the Glossary window displays a definition for the closest alphabetical match. Text above the definition box indicates which term is currently defined. In Figure R1.38a, the term *mean* is defined.

The Glossary window can be opened, closed, and moved. It cannot be resized.

Figure R1.38a *Glossary window*

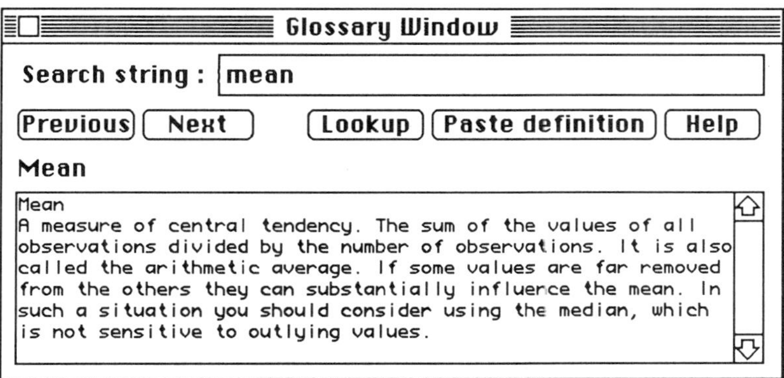

Note: You do not have to close the Glossary window to continue working. You can leave it open, move it, make another window active, and continue working.

R1.39 Requesting Definitions

The Glossary window works the same whether the Input window or the Output window is active.

- When you first open the Glossary window, it defines the term at the current insertion point in the active window. If there is no term at the insertion point, the **Search Entry** text box is blank, and the definition box asks you to type in a term.

- To request the definition of a term, type the term into the **Search Entry** text box. The Glossary window searches incrementally (that is, it immediately displays a definition when you begin typing, and continually defines the term that is the closest alphabetical match to whatever you have typed so far).

- As an alternative to typing a term in the **Search Entry** text box, you can select a term (drag over it) from either the Input or Output window. Click in the Glossary window to make it active, and then click the **Lookup** button to enter the selection into the **Search Entry** text box. You can select the term before you open the Glossary window or while the window is open. If the Glossary window is open, you may have to move it out of the way to select a term in the Input or Output window. If you click in the Input or Output window to make it active, it may obscure the Glossary window. To bring it back to the front, choose **Glossary Window** from the **Window** menu.

Buttons.   The following buttons are available for looking up terms in the Glossary window:

- **Lookup** pastes a selected term into the **Search Entry** text box and displays a definition. If some text in the active window is selected, **Lookup** uses that text as the selected term. If nothing is selected in the active window, **Lookup** uses the term containing the insertion point in the active window as the selected term.
- **Prev.** displays the glossary entry previous to the term currently defined.
- **Next** displays the glossary entry that follows the term currently defined.

R1.40 Pasting Definitions into the Active Window

To paste the Glossary window's current definition into the active window:

❻ Position the insertion point on the line just before the line where you want the entry to go.

❼ Click in the Glossary window (or select it from the **Window** menu) and then click the **Paste definition** button. This pastes the entire definition into the active window, beginning on the line below the insertion point.

R1.41 Closing the Glossary Window

To close the Glossary window, click the close box.

R1.42 Variables Window

Variables Window opens and closes the Variables window (Figure R.142a). Use it to see the names and labels of variables on the active SPSS system file or to paste variable names into the Input window. SPSS opens the Variables window automatically from the Command Generator whenever you paste into the Input window a selection that requires at least one variable name as an argument.

Each variable may also have value labels, assigned by either the VALUE LABELS or the ADD VALUE LABELS command (**read or write data** menu in the Command Generator). To see current value labels, run a DISPLAY DICTIONARY command (**session control and info** menu).

Figure R1.42a *Variables window*

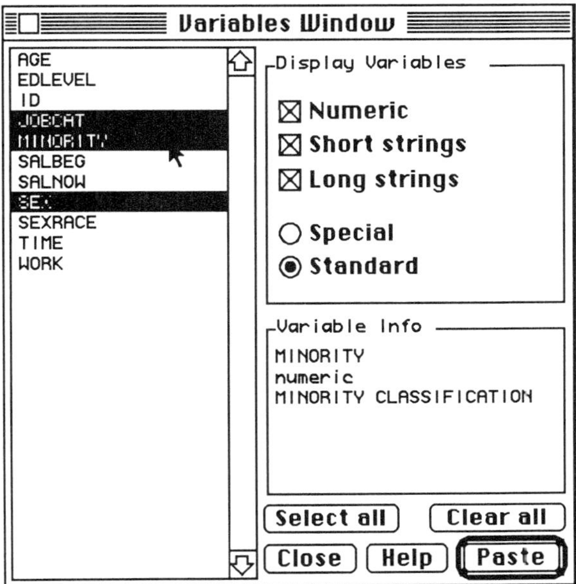

The Variables window can be moved but it cannot be resized. If you click in another window to make it active, the active window may obscure the Variables window. To bring it back to the front, choose **Variables Window** from the **Window** menu.

If you open the Variables window before you have defined the active SPSS system file, the list of variables is blank.

Display Options.   To specify the types of variable names displayed in the names box, use the **Display** options. By default, all standard variables are displayed. To remove any checked type, click its box:

- **Numerics** includes numeric variables in the names box.
- **Short strings** includes short string variables in the names box.
- **Long strings** includes long string variables in the names box.

Note: Display options affect only the variable names displayed. They *do not* affect the contents of the SPSS active system file.

If you deselect too many **Display** options, all variable names disappear from the names box. To retrieve the variable names in the names box, simply click the deselected check boxes.

Display Radio Buttons.   To determine the categories of variables displayed in the names box, use the **Display** radio buttons.

- **Special** displays only system variables and vector names in the names box. System variable names start with a dollar sign ($); these variables can be used in data transformation commands. These types of variables are discussed in the *SPSS Reference Guide.*
- **Standard** displays only the standard variables in the names box. These include permanent and temporary variables, but not system variables or vector names. This is the default.

Variables included in the display of standard or special variables depend on how the **Numerics, Short strings**, and **Long strings** check boxes are set. For example, if you deselect **Strings** when you select **Special Variables**, system and vector strings are not included in the names box.

R1.43 Looking Up Variable Names and Labels

To see the variable label for a variable, click that variable's name in the names box. The variable's label and type (numeric, string, or long string) are displayed in the **Variable Info** box. To see labels for other variables, press the up or down arrow key to move to the variable whose label you want to see.

Regardless of how many variable names are selected in the names box, the **Variable Info** box displays only one label at a time.

R1.44 Selecting Variable Names for Pasting

To select individual variables, click each variable name in the names box. To deselect the variable, select another variable. To select more than one variable at a time, press the Command key while you click the variable names. To select several contiguous variables, hold the Shift key while you drag down the list.

To select all variables displayed in the names box, click **Select All**. Once all variables are selected, you can deselect an individual variable by holding down the Command key and clicking its name in the list. To deselect all selected variables, click **Clear All.**

If variable names are selected in the names box but not pasted into the Input window, they remain selected. Thus, if you close the Variables window and open it later in the session, the same variables are still selected.

R1.45 Pasting Variable Names

There are two approaches to pasting variable names into the Input window:

- You can paste variable names individually. Use this approach to control the order in which variables are pasted (for example, for a VARIABLES specification on the REPORT command).
- You can paste a selected set of variable names. This approach is faster. Use it to paste variable names into the Input window in the same order as they appear in the names box.

To paste an individual variable name, double-click the variable name in the names box. Alternatively, select the variable name in the names box, and then click **Paste.** The window will close and you must open it again to paste another variable. To paste a set of variable names, select the names you want to paste and then click **Paste.**

Variable names that are pasted into the Input window wrap automatically to another line if they would cause the current command line to be too long.

Note: Variable names are pasted into the Input window at the insertion point or, if the insertion point is within a word, in front of the next delimiter. (See Universals in the *SPSS Reference Guide* for an explanation of delimiters.) Be sure the insertion point is positioned where you want the variable names to go.

R1.46 Clipboard Window

Clipboard Window shows the contents of the Clipboard. Information is written to the Clipboard when you use either the **Cut** or **Copy** option. The information remains on the Clipboard until you cut or copy something else. Sometimes the information on the Clipboard was placed there by an application program other than SPSS. It is in ASCII format.

R1.47 Output Window

Output Window makes the Output window active. From this window you can browse and edit output. If you have saved the Output window, its complete title is in the title bar, including the disk drive and folders above it in the hierarchy. The Output window can be moved, resized, or maximized.

R1.48 Input Window

Input Window [filename] makes the Input window active. In this window you can enter and run commands. If you have more than one Input window open, the open windows are listed on the menu by title. The active window title is indicated by a filled-in diamond shape. When all Input windows are closed, this option is not on the menu. An Input window can be moved, resized, or maximized.

R1.49 HELP MENU

Help displays a list of topics about using SPSS for the Macintosh and syntax of SPSS commands.

Figure R1.49a *Help menu*

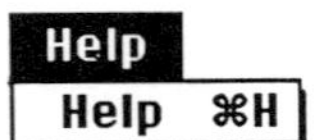

If an SPSS window is active when you choose **Help,** the topic selected concerns the active window (see Figure R1.49b). If you scroll through the list box on the left, first is a list of tasks and menu titles and then a list of SPSS commands. If you select a task or menu title, an explanation appears in the box on the right.

If you select an SPSS command, the syntax for that command appears (see Figure R1.49c). Explanations of syntax are in the *SPSS Reference Guide.*

Figure R1.49b *Help window*

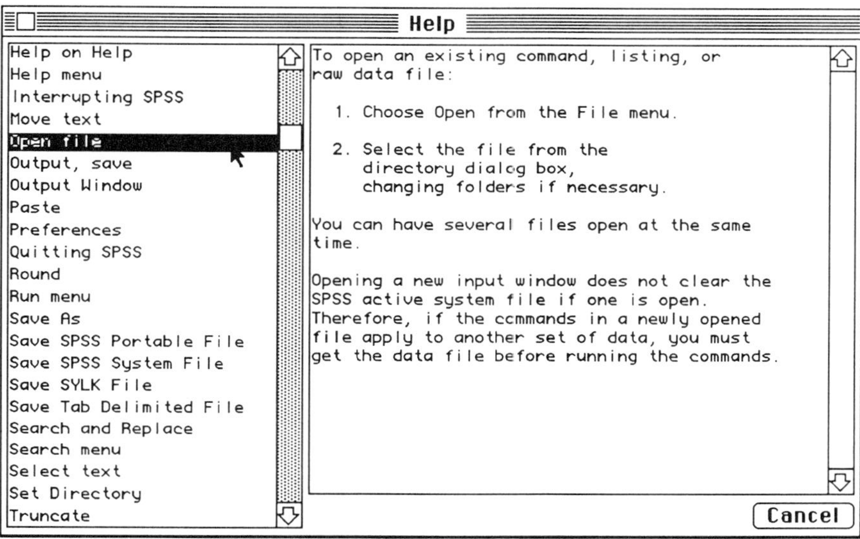

Figure R1.49c *Syntax charts online*

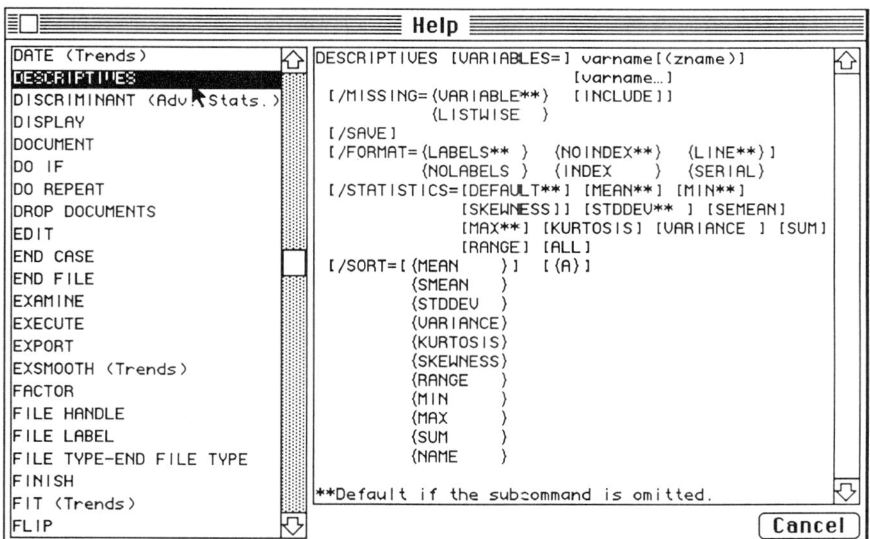

Running SPSS for the Macintosh

This chapter is a reference on how to perform various tasks in an SPSS session on the Macintosh. The major topics are in alphabetical order.

- Beginning an SPSS session (including customizing preferences).
- Commands.
- Command files.
- Data files.
- Help.
- Output (listing) files.
- Quitting a session.
- Selecting or saving files.

R2.1 BEGINNING AN SPSS SESSION

You can begin an SPSS session by opening the **SPSS** application.

❶ Click the **SPSS** icon (Figure R2.1a).

❷ Choose **Open** from the **File** menu.

As an alternative, you can double-click the SPSS icon.

Figure R2.1a *SPSS icon*

SPSS

R2.2 Customizing the Session

You can customize your session by choosing **Preferences** from the **Edit** menu. To make changes in preferences just before you start a new session, double-click the SPSS icon and then press and hold the mouse button until the **Preferences** dialog box appears. The preferences you enter at this time will be in effect for the current session and subsequent sessions.

If you make changes in the workspace or window width *during* a session, they affect only subsequent sessions, not the current one.

R2.3 Workspace

By default, SPSS allocates the optimum workspace based on the available memory. This allocation is enough workspace for running most procedures on a moderate-size data file.

In some circumstances, SPSS requires more workspace. For example, you may want to request a large number of transformations or run a sizable number of crosstabulations. SPSS sometimes displays messages to indicate that you must allocate more workspace to run a particular job. If you are doing a large number of transformations and you get a message that the job cannot be completed because of insufficient workspace, you can estimate how much space is needed. In a set of transformations, if about half the transformations were done before the message appeared, you can double the amount of workspace. Some messages tell you how much more workspace is needed.

You can assign more workspace to the session by typing in the number of kilobytes you need. The maximum amount of workspace you can request depends on the amount of memory installed, the amount of memory allocated to the Finder, and whether or not you are using the MultiFinder. If you attempt to allocate more workspace than available memory allows, SPSS displays an alert box telling you the maximum you can specify.

For example,

```
1500
```

allocates 1.5 megabytes of workspace for the session. If you want SPSS to allocate the optimum workspace based on the available memory, click the **Auto** check box.

R2.4 Rearrangement of Windows

By default, whenever you open the Command Generator window, the Input window jumps to the bottom of the screen at full width in front of the Output window. It jumps back when the Command Generator window closes. You can instruct SPSS to leave the Input window where you put it for this session; to do so, click the check box to the left of **Rearrange windows.**

R2.5 Window Width

You can select the width of the Input and Output windows by checking the appropriate box.

- **Standard** width accommodates approximately 80 characters of 9-point SPSSfont. If you have MultiFinder on, this width allows you to access the desktop behind the Input window.
- **Wide** accommodates approximately 132 characters of 9-point SPSSfont.
- **Maximized** indicates that each newly opened window will use the maximum width available on your monitor.

If you have a small monitor and choose **Wide** or **Maximized**, SPSS ignores the preference and uses **Standard** width.

R2.6 Storage of Temporary Files

You can specify the folder to store temporary files that SPSS creates during a session. Normally, temporary files are deleted at the end of a session, but in abnormal circumstances, such files can remain on the disk. If you don't want them in your System Folder, you can change to the SPSS application folder by checking the appropriate radio button.

- **System Folder** puts temporary files in the Macintosh System folder. This is the default.
- **Application Folder** puts temporary files in the folder that has the *SPSS application icon.*

R2.7 Closing the Preferences Box

Click the **OK** button when you are satisfied with your choices. **Cancel** closes the dialog box without making any changes.

R2.8 COMMANDS

In SPSS for the Macintosh, you enter and run commands from an Input window. When you save commands from an Input window, you create an SPSS command file.

R2.9 Entering Commands

To enter SPSS commands into an Input window during a session, you can

- Select and *paste* commands from SPSS menus in the Command Generator.
- Type commands directly into the window.
- Load commands from existing SPSS command files.

Usually you will use a combination of these methods during a session.
The following rules apply:

- Commands and subcommands can be indented and aligned to make them easier to read; they can also be abbreviated. The exception is END DATA, which must begin in column 1, must have a single space between END and DATA, and must be spelled out in full.
- Commands must end with a period. Exceptions are the BEGIN DATA and FINISH commands.

See the *SPSS Reference Guide* for additional rules governing the syntax of SPSS commands.

R2.10 Navigating Command Generator Menus

To open the Command Generator window, choose **Command Generator** from the **Window** menu. You may have to scroll through the Command Generator window to find the item you want.

- Click to select a menu item.
- As an alternative, press the Up or Down arrow key to move the highlight.

The description window on the right describes the selected item.

Moving Down the Menu Levels.   To proceed to the next menu level under a selection, do any of the following:

- Click **Next.** If the selection is one that can be pasted into the Input window, it is kept in a holding area in case you want to paste it later (see Section R2.11).
- Press the Right Arrow key to move down one level of menus. This is equivalent to clicking **Next.**
- Click **Paste.** If the selection is one that can be pasted, it is pasted directly into the Input window, including any higher levels not already pasted from the holding area.
- Double-click the selection. This is equivalent to clicking **Paste,** if available, or **Next** if **Paste** is dimmed.

A quick way to get to the menu level you want is to type as much of a command as you can remember into the Input window *before* you open the SPSS Command Generator window. The Command Generator window will then open at the appropriate menu for continuing with the command.

Moving Up the Menu Hierarchy.   To move back up the menu hierarchy, do any of the following:

- Click **Prev.** (previous) to return to the menu level above the current selection. If a selection was entered into the holding area in order to reach this level, that selection is removed from the holding area.
- Pressing the Left arrow key is equivalent to clicking **Prev.**
- To move to an SPSS menu at any level above the current menu, move the pointer to the current menu title and press the mouse button. A list of menus in the hierarchy appears, similar to the list that you can pull down in a directory dialog box. Drag to the menu you want and release the mouse button (see Figure R2.10a). Selections at all lower levels are removed from the holding area.

Figure R2.10a *Menu levels*

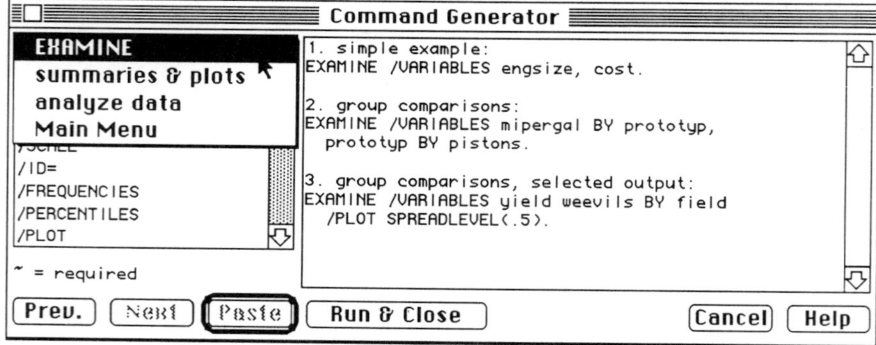

Exploring the Menus without Pasting.   To explore the SPSS menus without pasting selections into the Input window, use **Next.** When you click **Next,** the selection is entered into the holding area. It is removed from the holding area if you click **Prev.** to return to the level at which it was selected.

The holding area collects only selections that are in uppercase on the menus (these are commands or parts of commands). Selections are collected in the order they are entered by **Next.**

The advantages of exploring menus with **Next** are

- You can review lower-level selections without having to paste higher-level selections.

- You can collect selections in the holding area and then paste them together into the Input window. This reduces the chances of making syntax errors.
- It is quicker to remove a selection from the holding area than to delete it from the Input window.

When you reach the lowest level for your selections, the **Next** button is dimmed. You must then click **Paste** to paste selections from the holding area or click **Prev.** to remove the last selection that was entered into the holding area. You can also move up the hierarchy by pulling down the list of levels from the menu title and choosing the level you want.

R2.11 Pasting Selections

Menu selections that are in uppercase can be entered into the Input window by pasting them in. Before pasting, be sure the insertion point is positioned where you want the selection to go in the Input window.

- Command names are always pasted into the Input window at the beginning of the next line after the period at the end of the current command (the current command is the one containing the insertion point). If another command already exists on that line, it is moved down to make room for the command being pasted.
- SPSS subcommands and keywords are pasted into the Input window to the right of the word containing the insertion point, shifting everything else on the line to the right.
- Selections that are pasted from the Command Generator window wrap automatically if they would otherwise make a command line too long.
- The Command Generator lets you paste specifications where you want them and in the order you choose; it does not check for correct syntax until you run a command. If command syntax is incorrect, SPSS generates a warning or error message, which appears in the Output window.
- The Command Generator window automatically opens the Variables window if you paste a selection that requires at least one variable name as an argument.
- If you paste the BEGIN DATA command into the Input window, SPSS automatically pastes the END DATA command for you, and positions the insertion point between the two so you can begin typing data. A period is not pasted after BEGIN DATA, so SPSS will treat BEGIN DATA, END DATA, and any lines between them, as one continuous command rather than two separate commands.

- The Command Generator automatically adds apostrophes and parentheses to selections that require them. Whenever a filename is pasted from a dialog box, SPSS includes apostrophes and the full pathname, indicating the disk and folders as well as the document name.

To paste a selection from a menu into the Input window:

❶ Click **Paste.** You can also double-click the selection. This pastes the selection into the Input window and proceeds to the next menu level (if any).

❷ If the command is complete, you can run it. If not, paste any additional selections you need. If necessary, click **Prev.** to return to a higher-level menu.

❸ Continue moving up and down through menu levels, choosing and pasting selections until your command is complete.

R2.12 Typing Commands

When the Input window is active, you can type commands directly into it, even if the Command Generator window is open. To make an Input window active, use one of the following methods:

- Click the pointer anywhere within the Input window.
- Open the **Window** menu and then choose the name of the Input window you want.

Once the Input window is active, you can type as many new command lines as you like, edit commands currently in the window, or reposition the insertion point for pasting selections from the menus. To return to the SPSS command menus, click in the Command Generator window, or press Command-M.

As a general rule, it is easier to use the Command Generator for entering commands that process data (for example, those that perform a statistical analysis, or produce a report, listing, or plot). Commands that are highly customized, such as commands that describe your data file (for example, those that assign labels and formats to the data) or modify your data (for example, those that consolidate values into categories or compute new values from existing values), are easier to type.

R2.13 Loading Commands from a File

To load commands into an Input window from an existing file:

❶ Choose **Open** from the **File** menu. A directory dialog box appears.

❷ Select a file.

❸ Click the **Open** button. A new Input window opens, containing the text in the file.

R2.14 Running the Commands

Entering a command into the Input window does not run it. You must instruct SPSS to run commands. First, either position the insertion point within a command or select one or more commands. Then run the commands in any of the following ways:

- Click the **Run & Close** button in the Command Generator window. In addition to running the selected commands, **Run & Close** closes the Command Generator window.
- Choose **Run Selection** from the **Run** menu. **Run Selection** is available only when the Input window is active. As an alternative to choosing **Run Selection,** press the keyboard equivalent Command-R. **Run Selection** does not close the Command Generator window.
- Press the Enter key. This has the same effect as choosing **Run Selection.**

Before you run a command, be sure it is complete and that its syntax is correct (see Section R2.9).

- If you run a command that does not have a period, a dialog box informs you that the period is missing. You must then close the dialog box by clicking **OK,** type a period at the end of the command, and run it again. Exceptions are BEGIN DATA and FINISH, which do not require a period. It is usually best to omit the period on BEGIN DATA so that when you select or run the commands, the whole sequence BEGIN DATA—END DATA is treated as a single command rather than two separate commands.

Caution: To find the beginning of a command, SPSS searches up in the Input window from the insertion point until it finds a period. It then uses the line below the period as the first line of the current command. If the period is missing on the previous command, SPSS merges the previous command with the current command, and a syntax error results.

- If no text is selected, SPSS runs only the command containing the insertion point. The insertion point can be anywhere within the command. For example, if the command occupies three lines in the Input window, the insertion point can be positioned anywhere on those three lines.

- To run more than one command, select the commands before clicking the button or pressing the Enter key. All the selected commands are run sequentially, as though they were run one at a time.

R2.15 Interrupting Commands That Are Running

You can interrupt command processing at any time (that is, you can stop commands that are running) by clicking the **Cancel** button in the status dialog box.

Following an interruption, you may want to check the data dictionary and data transformations in the active SPSS system file to see what has been updated. If a complete data pass did not occur prior to the attention interrupt, there may be no SPSS active system file following the interrupt. This might be the case if none of the prior commands caused the data to be read. (Data definition and transformation commands such as DATA LIST, VALUE LABELS, COMPUTE, and RECODE do not cause the data to be read. See the *SPSS Reference Guide* for a list of the commands that cause the data to be read.)

R2.16 Viewing and Editing Output

When you run a command, output written to the Output window scrolls continuously (if necessary). The output contains the commands that have been run, results of running the commands, and messages from SPSS about processing, including error messages.

You can edit text in the Output window. If you want to preserve the original output, be sure to save the file before editing.

R2.17 COMMAND FILES

When you begin a session, SPSS opens an empty, untitled Input window. This empty window is essentially a temporary command file. If you enter any commands into this file, the command file is not created on disk unless you explicitly save it.

R2.18 Creating New Command Files

The best way to create a new command file is to Choose **New** from the **File** menu. **New** opens a new, untitled window. Other Input windows remain open.

Opening a new Input window does not clear the active SPSS system file if one is open. The new command file is opened in the new Input window. To create the file on disk, you must save it after you enter your commands.

As an alternative to creating a command file within SPSS, you can use a text editor or word processor to create the command file. The editor or word processor must save the file in ASCII (text-only) format so SPSS can read it. Choose **Text Only** in your word processor, or copy the text to the Clipboard and paste it into the SPSS Input window.

R2.19 Opening Existing Command Files

You can open a command file either within a session or directly from the Macintosh desktop.

R2.20 Opening a Command File during an SPSS Session

To open an existing command file:

❶ Choose **Open** from the **File** menu. A directory dialog box appears.

❷ Select the filename and click the **Open** button or double-click the filename.

During a session, **Open** opens another Input window and loads commands from an existing file into the new Input window. This does not clear the active SPSS system file if one is open.

Open can be used at the start of a new session. It can also be used during a session to access commands from an external file.

R2.21 Opening a Command File from the Desktop

You can open a command file from the Macintosh desktop if it is in the same folder as the SPSS application.

❶ Click the file icon to select it.

❷ Hold down the Shift key and click the SPSS application icon. This leaves both applications selected.

❸ Choose **Open** from the **File** menu (or double-click the file icon). This starts an SPSS session and automatically loads the command file into the Input window.

Note: To run commands in the command file, you must define data for SPSS. Before running the commands, check to see if there is a GET command or a DATA LIST, or similar command as the first command in the file. If there is not a command for defining data, either add one at the beginning of the file or choose **Get SPSS System File** or **Get Data File** from the **File** menu.

R2.22 Saving Command Files

To save commands that are in the Input window:

❶ Make the Input window active.

❷ Choose either **Save** or **Save As** from the **File** menu.

R2.23 DATA FILES

To perform an analysis you need data. In SPSS for the Macintosh, your data can come from any of the following sources:

- **SPSS system files**, which are files created by choosing **Save SPSS System File** from the **File** menu, or by running the SAVE command. System files can also be created with the XSAVE command.

- **SPSS portable files,** which are files created by choosing **Save Data File** from the **File** menu, or by running the SPSS EXPORT command. By storing files in portable format, you can use them in SPSS on another operating system. For example, portable files created in SPSS for the Macintosh can be used in SPSS/PC+ on DOS machines, and vice versa.

- **SYLK files,** which are created by Microsoft Excel using SYLK (Microsoft symbolic link) format.

- **Multiplan spreadsheet files,** which are created by Microsoft symbolic link (SYLK).

- **Tab-delimited files,** which are created by many spreadsheet and database applications. These files have tabs between data items and carriage returns at the ends of lines.

- **Raw data files** created by a text editor or word processor.

- **Column binary (multipunch) data.**

Sections R2.24 through R2.26 and R2.29 through R2.31 describe how to read and save SPSS system files, portable files, dBASE files, Excel files, and Multiplan files. See Section R2.27 for information on raw data files, and Section R2.28 for information on column binary data.

R2.24 Getting Data Files

SPSS system files, SPSS portable files, and SYLK spreadsheet files contain data plus descriptive information about the data. They are in a format you cannot read or edit with a text editor or word processor.

You can get a data file in any of the following ways:

- To get a data file without entering a GET, GET TRANSLATE or IMPORT command into the Input window, choose the **Get** command from the **File** menu. After you select the file, click **Get** in the dialog box. **Get** automatically runs the default setting for GET (when you get SPSS system files), GET TRANSLATE (when you get Excel or Multiplan SYLK files, or tab-delimited files), or IMPORT (when you get SPSS portable files). This is a quick, easy way to get data files.

- To get a data file by entering a GET, GET TRANSLATE or IMPORT command into the Input window, use the **File** menu. After you select the file to get, click **Paste** in the dialog box. This enters the default setting for the GET, GET TRANSLATE, or IMPORT command into the Input window and selects it, but does not run it.
- As an alternative to using the **File** menu, you can type the command or select and paste it from the **Command Generator.**

The last two methods require you to instruct SPSS to run the command. With these two methods, you can add subcommands to perform additional functions, such as keeping, dropping, or renaming variables from the input file (see the *SPSS Reference Guide* for information on these additional functions). Because the command is in the Input window, you can save it along with the other commands in the file. The next time you use the command file you will already have a defined file specification.

R2.25 Getting SPSS System Files

To get an SPSS system file

❶ Open the **File** menu and drag to **Get SPSS System File.** This opens a directory dialog box.

❷ Select the file.

❸ Check **Get** in the dialog box.

Once you get the file, an SPSS active system file is created.

Get Command.   You can also get a system file by running a GET command with the FILE subcommand. For example,

```
GET FILE=Bank.SPSS-Sys.
```

gets the system file Bank.SPSS-Sys when you run it.

If the file is not in the *set* directory, you must specify the pathname, enclosing the entire file specification in apostrophes or quotation marks (see Section R2.32). You can also set the directory by choosing **Set Directory** from the **File** menu.

R2.26 Getting Other Data Files

To get an SPSS portable file, SYLK spreadsheet file, or tab-delimited file:

❶ Open the File menu, and drag to **Get Data File.** This opens a submenu of file types.

❷ Drag to the type of file you want and release the mouse button. This opens a directory dialog box listing files of the type you chose.

❸ Select the file and click the **Get** button.

Once you get the file, an SPSS active system file is created.

To read variable names from the first row of a range in the spreadsheet or tab-delimited file:

❹ Click in the check box for **Read Variable Names**.

To specify a range of columns in a spreadsheet file:

❺ Enter a range into the **Range** field. Separate the ranges with a colon, as in **R1C1:R14C11**.

IMPORT Command.   You can also get an SPSS portable file by running an IMPORT command with the FILE subcommand.

```
IMPORT FILE=CMSBank.por.
```

gets the portable file CMSBank.por.

If the file is not in the set directory, you must specify the pathname, enclosing the entire file specification in apostrophes or quotation marks (see Section R2.32). You can change the current directory by choosing **Set Directory** from the **File** menu.

GET TRANSLATE Command.   You can also get SYLK spreadsheet or tab-delimited files by running a GET TRANSLATE command with the FILE and TYPE subcommands. Specify the filename on the FILE subcommand, enclosing the file specification in apostrophes or quotes. For example,

```
GET TRANSLATE FILE='Budget.SYLK' /TYPE=SLK.
```

gets the file Budget.SYLK, whose type is identified by the TYPE subcommand. Note that SPSS uses the TYPE subcommand, not the file type on the file specification, to determine the type. The available specifications on TYPE are

SLK   *Excel or Multiplan file (symbolic format only).*
TAB   *Tab-delimited file.*

Reading Variable Names from SYLK and Tab-Delimited Files.   By default, SPSS does not read variable names from the first row of the range in a SYLK spreadsheet or tab-delimited file. Instead, it uses the names VAR1 to VARn. To read variable names, use the FIELDNAMES subcommand. For example, the command

```
GET TRANSLATE FILE='Budget.SYLK' /TYPE=SLK /FIELDNAMES.
```

creates an active SPSS system file from a SYLK spreadsheet file using the names in the first row as variable names.

Specifying Spreadsheet Ranges.   By default, SPSS gets the entire SYLK spreadsheet file. To get a specified range from the spreadsheet, use the RANGE subcommand. Use a colon to separate the beginning and end of the range, as in:

```
GET TRANSLATE FILE='MONTHLY.SLK' /TYPE=SLK /RANGE=R1C1:R14C11.
```

If you specify a range and fieldnames, variable names are read from the first row of the range.

R2.27 Reading Raw Data Files

Raw data files contain only data. They are in a format you can read or edit with a text editor or word processor. You should save them as "text only" files if entered in a word processor.

To read a raw data file, you must enter into the Input window a DATA LIST or similar command that assigns names to variables and provides information about the column locations and formats of the data, as in:

```
DATA LIST FILE=Value.Data
 /COMPANY 1-8(A) TYPE 10 PRICE 12-16(1) METHOD 18.
```

- The FILE subcommand indicates the data are in file Value.Data in the application folder or the folder set by a SET DIRECTORY command.
- Variable COMPANY is alphanumeric. Variables TYPE, PRICE, and METHOD are numeric (the default). Variable PRICE has one decimal position.

When you run the DATA LIST (or similar) command, an SPSS active system file is built by combining

- Data from the raw data file.
- Information you supply on the DATA LIST (or similar) command.
- Information on any data definition and transformation commands you run.

The original data file is unaffected, even if you save the data in a system file. See the *SPSS Base System User's Guide* for more information on defining data in SPSS.

R2.28 Reading Fixed Record-Length or Multipunch Files

To read files with records longer than 1024 bytes, multipunch (column binary) files, and fixed record-length files, you must use the FILE HANDLE command to assign a *handle* to the file. The FILE HANDLE command must precede the first reference to the file. You can then refer to that file by its handle on a DATA LIST or similar command.

The syntax for FILE HANDLE is

```
FILE HANDLE handle/
        NAME='filename'
        [LRECL=record length]
        [MODE={MULTIPUNCH}]
              {IMAGE    }
```

- The handle can be any name you choose as long as it conforms to the rules for SPSS variable names: it must start with a letter, contain only letters, digits, or one of the characters $, #, @, and _, and cannot exceed eight characters. The handle INLINE is reserved and refers to data read from the command file. Do not attempt to redefine that handle.
- The apostrophes (or quotes) on the NAME subcommand are required.

Keywords for the MODE subcommand are

IMAGE   *Files with fixed record lengths.* LRECL must also be specified with these files.

MULTIPUNCH   *Files with 160-byte records that are the images of 80-column cards.* Only input commands (DATA LIST and similar commands) can use multipunch files. Because their record length is fixed at 160, LRECL is not required with these files.

For example,

```
FILE HANDLE  applbuyr/ NAME='U2:Marketing:AppleBuyers'
                       MODE=MULTIPUNCH.
DATA LIST FILE=applbuyr /...
```

assigns the handle applbuyr to the file AppleBuyers, which is located in the directory Marketing folder on disk drive U2. The handle applbuyr is then specified on DATA LIST. The MODE subcommand indicates the data are multipunch. The command

```
FILE HANDLE  nmrdata/ NAME='NMR Data' MODE=IMAGE LRECL=16.
```

assigns the handle nmrdata to the file NMR Data. The FILE HANDLE command is required because the file is not a text file but an image file where each record is 16 bytes long.

R2.29 Saving Data Files

You can save SPSS data files into various types of files that contain the data plus descriptive information about the data. These files are in a format that you cannot read or edit with a text editor or word processor.

- To save a data file without entering a SAVE, SAVE TRANSLATE or EXPORT command into the Input window, choose a **Save** command from the **File** menu. After you select the type of file to save, click the **Save** button in the dialog box. The **Save** button automatically runs the default setting for SAVE (when you save SPSS system files), SAVE TRANSLATE (when you save SYLK or tab-delimited files), or EXPORT (when you save SPSS portable files). This is a quick, easy way to save data files.

- To save a data file by entering a SAVE, SAVE TRANSLATE or EXPORT command into the Input window, use the **File** menu and the **Paste** button. Be sure the insertion point is positioned where you want the command pasted. After you select the file to save, click **Paste** in the dialog box. This enters the default setting for the SAVE, SAVE TRANSLATE, or EXPORT command into the Input window and selects it. You must then run the command.

- As an alternative to using the **File** menu, you can type the command or select and paste it from the Command Generator window. You must then run the command.

With the last two methods you can add subcommands to perform additional functions, such as keeping, dropping, or renaming variables from the input file (see the *SPSS Reference Guide* for information on these additional functions).

Note: When you end a session, SPSS *does not* query whether you want to save the data file. If you run any data definition or transformation commands during a session or any procedures that create new variables during a session, the SPSS active system file contains those changes. The original data file you opened to begin the analysis does not contain those changes. To store the changes, you must save the data file, either as an SPSS system file or in one of the other data formats.

R2.30 Saving SPSS System Files

To save an SPSS system file

❶ Open the **File** menu.

❷ Choose **Save SPSS System File.** This opens a dialog box so you can name the file. You can use any filename valid on the Macintosh, including those with blanks.

❸ Click **Save** in the dialog box.

SAVE Command.   You can also save an SPSS system file by running a SAVE or XSAVE command with the OUTFILE subcommand. For example,

```
SAVE OUTFILE=Bank.SPSS-Sys.
```

saves the system file Bank.SPSS-Sys.

By default, the file is saved in the directory determined by the SET DIRECTO-RY command (available on the **File** menu). To specify an alternative folder, you must enclose the entire file specification in apostrophes or quotation marks (see Section R2.32) or choose **Set Directory** from the **File** menu. You must also use apostrophes or quotes if there is a blank in the filename.

R2.31 Saving Other Data Files

To save an SPSS portable file, SYLK spreadsheet file, or tab-delimited file:

❶ Open the **File** menu and then choose **Save Data File.** This opens a submenu that lets you choose the type of file.

❷ Choose the type of file to save. This opens a dialog box so you can name the file.

Caution: For spreadsheet and tab-delimited files, save the file under a new name instead of its original name. SPSS discards information such as formulas and range names when it saves the file. If you save it under the old name, those items will be lost in the original file.

❸ If you want to save variable names in the spreadsheet or tab-delimited file, click the check box to the left of **Write variable names.**

EXPORT Command.   You can also save files as SPSS portable files by running an EXPORT command with the OUTFILE subcommand. For example,

```
EXPORT OUTFILE=CMSBank.Por.
```

saves the portable file CMSBank.Por.

By default, the file is saved in the set directory. To specify an alternative directory, you must enclose the entire file specification in apostrophes or quotation marks (see Section R2.32).

SAVE TRANSLATE Command.   You can also save files as SYLK spreadsheet or tab-delimited files by running a SAVE TRANSLATE command with the OUTFILE subcommand. Specify the filename on OUTFILE, enclosing the file specification in apostrophes or quotes. For example,

```
SAVE TRANSLATE OUTFILE='Budget.SYLK' /TYPE=SLK.
```

saves the file Budget.SYLK as a SYLK file, as indicated on the TYPE subcommand. The specifications available for the TYPE subcommand are:

SLK   *Excel or Multiplan file (symbolic format only).*

TAB   *Tab-delimited file.*

By default, the file is saved in the set directory. To save the file in a different directory (folder), include the pathname on the file specification or change the directory by running a SET DIRECTORY command.

Saving Variable Names.   By default, SPSS does not save variable names as the first row of the range in a spreadsheet file. To save variable names, use the FIELDNAMES subcommand. For example,

```
SAVE TRANSLATE OUTFILE=Budget.SLK /TYPE=SLK /FIELDNAMES.
```

saves a SYLK file. The variable names defined in SPSS are used as fieldnames for the first row in the spreadsheet (see the *SPSS Reference Guide).*

R2.32   Referring to Files on SPSS Commands

In SPSS, you either select files from directory dialog boxes or specify them directly on a command. Depending on the command and whether you are reading or writing a file, you use either a FILE, OUTFILE, MATRIX, or WRITE subcommand to refer to the file. You can specify the file in one of two ways:

- Specify only a filename in the command and set the directory to the folder that contains the file.
- Specify the full pathname.

If a filename contains blanks or special characters, you must enclose it in apostrophes.

Specifying a File in the Set Directory.   If a file is in the set directory, you can simply type the filename on the subcommand. For example, suppose the file Value.Data is in the Value folder within the SPSS 4.0 folder on disk drive UserHD. If you started SPSS from the SPSS 4.0 folder, that is the default directory, no matter what folder you made *current* in opening the file Value.Commands. Even if the Value folder is current, you must still set the directory to the Value folder before running the following command:

```
DATA LIST FILE=Value.Data /...
```

Otherwise, SPSS will not be able to find Value.Data in the SPSS 4.0 folder and will issue an error. Similarly, a command that produces output, such as

```
REPORT FORMAT=AUTOMATIC LIST
  /VARIABLES=NAME DEPT TITLE SALARY
  /OUTFILE=Personnel.Listing.
```

writes the file Personnel.Listing to the set directory.

To set the directory

❶ Choose **Set Directory** from the **File** menu.

❷ Since the current folder is Value, click the **Set This Directory** button. You can then proceed with running the command.

If you select another directory in the **Set Directory** dialog box, the current directory for opening files is also changed.

Alternatively, you can run a SET DIRECTORY command, using the full pathname of the folder.

Specifying a Pathname.   If a file is not in the set directory, you must specify the pathname, enclosing the entire file specification in apostrophes or quotation marks. A pathname indicates the entire file hierarchy for finding a file. First is the disk name, then the folder name at each level, and finally the filename. The levels are separated by colons. The format is

```
diskname:folder1:folder2:...:filename
```

You can use the **Find File** desk accessory to determine the details of the pathname. If the pathname includes an apostrophe, enclose the pathname in quotation marks. The **Find File** dialog box is shown in Figure R2.32a.

Figure R2.32a *Find File dialog box*

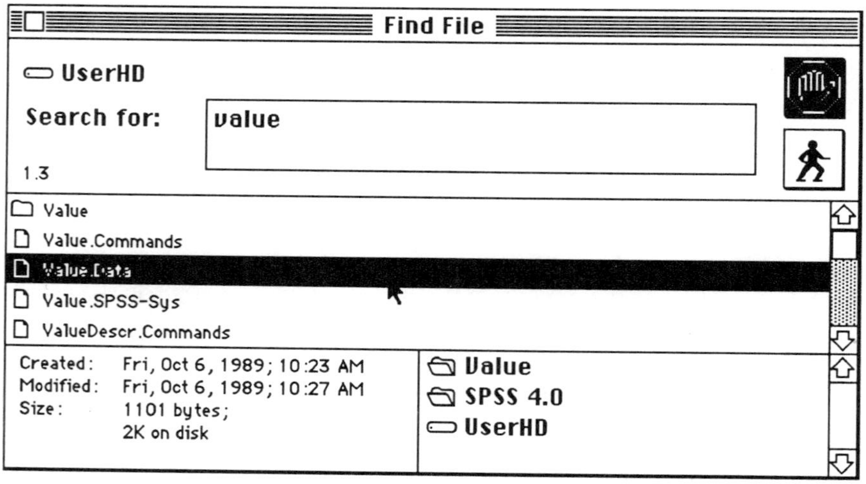

For example,

```
DATA LIST FILE='UserHD:SPSS 4.0:Value:Value.Data' /...
```

indicates data are located in the file UserHD:SPSS 4.0:Value:Value.Data, where SPSS 4.0 and Value are folders on the disk drive UserHD.

If the pathname is very long, you may want to assign a file handle, using the FILE HANDLE command.

R2.33 HELP

The following online help is available:

- Help for using SPSS. This help includes online syntax charts for SPSS commands.
- SPSS command descriptions and examples.
- Glossary (see Chapter R1).

R2.34 Help for SPSS

To get help for any SPSS window or dialog box that pops up on your screen, choose **Help** from the **Help** menu or press Command-H. The help window that opens instructs you on how to use the current window or dialog box. You may have to scroll through the help window to read all the instructions.

Note: You do not have to close the help window to continue working. You can leave it open, resize and move it if you like, make another window active, and continue working.

- The **Cancel** button closes the Help window.

R2.35 Online Syntax Charts

If you scroll down the contents of the Help list, the second part contains a complete syntax chart for every SPSS command. You can easily check a command for requirements, subcommand order, or other details before running it.

R2.36 SPSS Command Descriptions and Examples

To see descriptions and examples for SPSS commands:

❶ Choose **Command Generator** from the **Window** menu. This opens the Command Generator window. The SPSS menu on the left lets you make selections. The description window on the right describes the current selection.

❷ Select an item on the menu and read the text in the description window.

❸ Click the **Next** button and proceed through menu levels until you reach the selection for which you need help.

If you know the command you want to use but cannot remember its syntax:

❶ Position the insertion point in the Input window on the command for which you want help. If you have not yet entered the command, begin a new line and type as much of the command as you can remember into the Input window.

❷ Open the Command Generator window. The description window opens at the appropriate level for the command at the current insertion point.

❸ Select the keyword for which you need help.

For example, if you type REGRESSION on a new line in the Input window and then open the Command Generator window, the description window opens at the subcommand level for REGRESSION. You can then select the keyword for which you need help.

R2.37 OUTPUT (LISTING) FILES

When you begin a session, SPSS opens an empty Output window. This window is essentially a temporary listing file. Output that is written to this window is not saved on disk unless you explicitly save it.

R2.38 Creating Listing Files

To create a new listing file:

❶ Make the Output window active.

❷ Choose **Select All** and then **Clear** from the **File** menu.

If you want to keep the old output file, be sure you save it before clearing.

R2.39 Opening Listing Files

To view an existing listing file:

❶ Choose **Open** from the **File** menu.

Select the file you want to see and click on **Open.** The listing file appears in the new Input window. If you want to, you can copy or cut lines and paste them into the Output window.

R2.40 Saving Output into Listing Files

When SPSS for the Macintosh writes output to the Output window, it does not automatically copy that output to a listing file. To save output into a listing file:

❶ Make the Output window active.

❷ Choose **Save As** from the **File** menu.

R2.41 QUITTING A SESSION

To quit a session, choose **Quit** from the **File** menu. If there is unsaved text in either the Output or Input window, a dialog box queries whether to save it.

R2.42 SELECTING OR SAVING FILES

When working with the **File** menu, you frequently select files to work with, or assign names to files you want to save. To select a file, you use a directory dialog box. To save a file, you use a directory dialog box that contains a text box for the name of the file. See your Macintosh documentation if you need more information about using directory dialog boxes than is given in the following sections.

R2.43 Types of Files

All SPSS directory dialog boxes work the same way; what differs is the type of files each displays in its list of files. For example, Figure R2.43a shows a sample of the dialog box that pops up when you choose **Open**. The box displays only files marked internally by SPSS as TEXT files.

Figure R2.43a *Dialog box for Open*

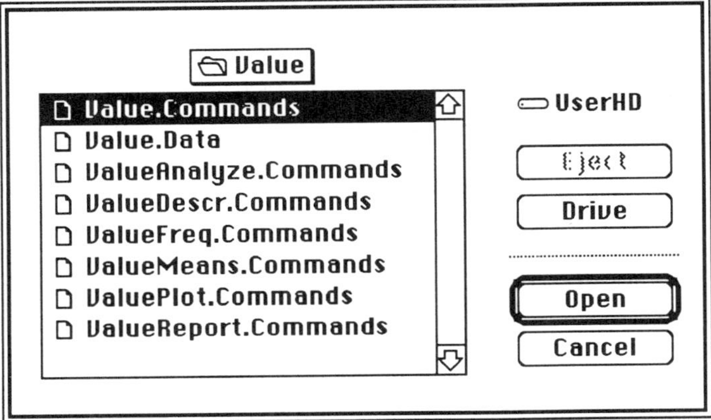

When files are saved in SPSS for the Macintosh, the program marks the file type internally. The following file types are listed in various dialog boxes.

TEXT *SPSS command file.* A document you create by saving the commands from the Input window.

TEXT *SPSS listing file.* A document you create when you save the contents from the Output window, or SPSS creates when you send procedure results to an external file with an OUTFILE, MATRIX, or WRITE subcommand.

TEXT *Tab-delimited files.* Tab-delimited files have a Tab character after each data element and a Return character at the end of each line. You can save tab-delimited files in many other applications. You can also create them in a word processing program, tabbing after each data entry and pressing Return at the end of each line.

TEXT *Text file.* A document created by saving from a word processor in **Text Only** format.

SYS *SPSS system file.* A file saved by choosing **Save SPSS System File** from the **File** menu. It contains data and a data dictionary readable by SPSS. You can also save SPSS system file by running an SPSS command SAVE or XSAVE.

SYLK *Symbolic format file.* A SYLK data file can be created in Multiplan or Excel by selecting SYLK when saving the file in that application. You can also save SPSS data files in the SYLK format.

R2.44 Directory Dialog Boxes

All SPSS directory dialog boxes have a directory title, list of contents, current disk name, and buttons similar to those described below. To select a file, you use one or more of these items. When you use any of the directory dialog boxes, first check to see if the current folder (identified in the directory title) is the folder that contains the file you want.

Figure R2.44a *Directory dialog box*

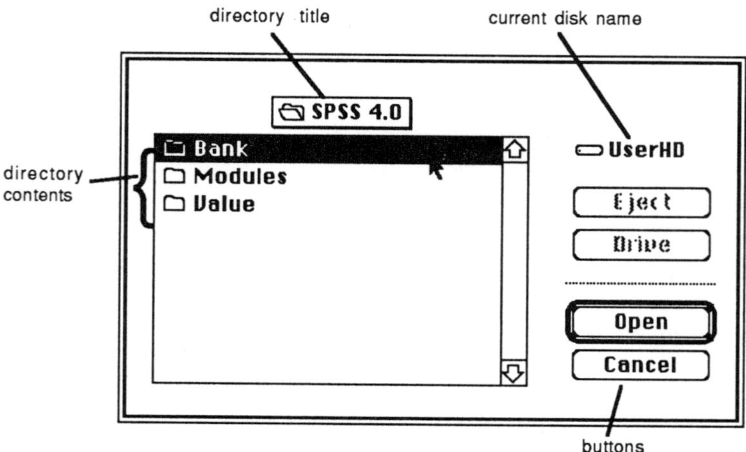

Note: If you change the current folder (or disk), the chosen folder becomes the current folder *for the rest of your session,* unless you change it again or set the directory.

R2.45 Directory Title

The title box shows the title of the directory. Typically a directory is a folder, but it can also be a disk name (hard disk or floppies). Files listed in the contents reside in this folder.

If the file you want is not in the current folder, you can open another folder in the list by selecting it and clicking the **Open** button or by double-clicking the folder you want to open. If you change the folder, the list of contents is refreshed automatically to show the files in the folder that is now current.

To see the hierarchical list of folders, move the pointer to the title of the current folder and press the mouse button. A pull-down list similar to a menu appears. You can choose a folder or drive by dragging the pointer to the title and releasing the mouse button.

To change from one drive to another, click the **Drive** button. The title of the other drive appears in the title box and the list of contents is refreshed. If there are more than two drives, click the **Drive** button again to access another drive. If the **Drive** button is dimmed, no other drive is available.

To eject a disk, click the **Eject** button. You can then insert another disk if you want to.

R2.46 Directory Contents

The list of files displayed in the directory contents are only those files in the current folder that correspond to the type of file you are selecting. For example, if you choose **Get SPSS System File** from the **File** menu, only folders and SPSS system files appear in the list.

The file you are looking for may not appear in the directory contents for one of the following reasons:

- The file is not recognized as the file type that SPSS uses to identify that type of file.
- The file is not in the current folder.

If you cannot find a file by looking in several folders, you may be able to locate it with the Macintosh desk accessory **Find File.**

R2.47 Current Disk Name

At the top on the right side of the dialog box is the icon and name of the current disk. If you click the icon, the directory moves up one level in the hierarchy of folders.

R2.48 Buttons

The buttons vary according to the selection window you are using. Generally, click the appropriate button to proceed with the file selection, or cancel the request.

R2.49 Selecting and Opening a File

To select and open a file from the list:

❶ Click the filename you want (you may have to scroll through the list to find the file).

❷ Once you select the file, click the appropriate button (**Open**, **Append**, or **Insert**, depending on the dialog box) to proceed with the file selection. As an alternative to clicking on the button, double-click the filename in the list.

If the file you are selecting is a data file, the selection window has a **Paste** button. As an alternative to clicking **Open** in Step 2, you can click **Paste**. Depending on the type of data file, this pastes a GET, GET TRANSLATE, or IMPORT command into the Input window. The command is automatically selected, but SPSS awaits your instructions before running it.

R2.50 Saving a File

To save the contents of the active window, you can choose either **Save** or **Save As** from the **File** menu. If you choose **Save**, changes made since the last **Save** or **Save As** overwrite the existing file on disk. If you choose **Save As**, a new file is created on disk, leaving the old file intact. Further **Save** commands overwrite the new file. The **Save As** dialog box (Figure R2.50a) saves everything in the active window. If the Input window or Output window is active, **Save As** saves the contents to a TEXT file.

Save As saves files in the current folder (identified in the title box), unless you first select a different folder, as described in Section R2.45.

Figure R2.50a *Dialog box for Save As*

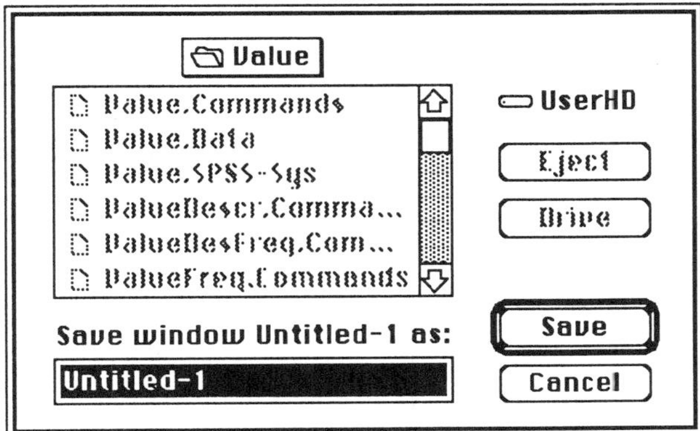

To save a file:

❶ Type the filename into the **Save [item]** text box. Be sure to change the folder if you do not want to save the file in the current folder. (The folder you choose becomes the folder for the rest of your session, unless you change it again later.)

❷ Click **Save.** If the filename you assign is unique, the file is saved. If the filename you assign already exists within the folder, a dialog box queries whether you want to replace the existing file:

- **Yes** saves the contents of the active window. Contents of the current file replace contents of the original file.

- **No** does not save the contents of the active window. If you still want to save the file, but under a new name, choose **Save As** again and this time assign a unique name to the file.

R2.51 Setting the Directory

You can change the directory before running an SPSS command containing a filename. Then you don't have to type the complete pathname for the file.

❶ Choose **Set Directory** from the **File** menu. The dialog box lists folders within the current directory.

❷ Click the appropriate button:

- **Select This Directory** selects the title directory just below the button.
- **Directory** selects the folder that is highlighted.
- **Open** opens the folder that is highlighted. Then you can proceed with selecting the directory.

You can also set the directory by running a SET DIRECTORY command. Either method of setting the directory also changes the current directory for standard directory dialog boxes.

Chapter R3

Text Editing in SPSS

SPSS provides all the editing features you need for working with SPSS command files and output (listing) files. Though you can use the SPSS editor to create, edit, or browse through any text file, it was not designed to replace your word processor.

The SPSS text editor follows the usual Macintosh conventions for editing text and also provides some special features for selecting commands. If you are familiar with text-editing on the Macintosh, you can skip Sections R3.1 through R3.14 and read about selecting text, starting with Section R3.15.

R3.1 USING THE INSERTION POINT

The insertion point (a blinking vertical line) indicates the position where text will be inserted or deleted, depending on the function you select.

R3.2 Moving the Insertion Point with the Mouse

To position the insertion point anywhere within the active window:

❶ Use the mouse to move the pointer where you want the insertion point to go.

❷ Click.

R3.3 Moving the Insertion Point with Keyboard Keys

In addition to moving the insertion point with the mouse, you can use arrow keys (sometimes called cursor keys). The following keys move the insertion point:

- The Right Arrow key moves the insertion point to the right one character.
- The Left Arrow key moves the insertion point to the left one character.
- Command- Right Arrow moves the insertion point to the end of the line.
- Command- Left Arrow moves the insertion point to the beginning of the line.
- The Up Arrow key moves the insertion point up one line.
- The Down Arrow key moves the insertion point down one line.
- The Tab key inserts blanks to the next tab stop, which is four characters to the right.

On the extended keyboard, the following key functions are available in addition to those listed above:

- The Page Up key moves the view up one screen and leaves the insertion point where it was. (You can also use the scroll bars to change the view.)
- The Page Down key moves the view down one screen and leaves the insertion point where it was.
- The Home key moves the insertion point to the top of the file.
- The End key moves the insertion point to the bottom of the file.

R3.4 EDITING TEXT

Both the Input and Output window have a maximum line length of 255 characters. Text you type into the window or paste with the **Paste** option on the **Edit** menu does not wrap automatically. However, text pasted from the SPSS Command Generator window wraps automatically if it would otherwise cause a command line to be too long.

Caution: When SPSS for Macintosh writes output to the Output window, it *does not* automatically copy that output to a listing file. Be sure to save contents of the Output window *before* you make any modifications; you *can* undo only the most recent editing change you made.

Sections R3.5 through R3.14 provide an alphabetical reference to the editing functions you can perform with the SPSS editor.

R3.5 Adding New Lines

To add a line above the current line:

❶ Move the pointer to the beginning of the line and click.

❷ Press Return.

To add a line below the current line:

❶ Move the pointer to the end of the line and click.

❷ Press Return.

R3.6 Appending Text to the End of a File

To append text to the end of a file, you do not open the file to which you want to add the text. Rather, you copy text from the active window to the end of the existing file:

❶ To append only selected text, select the text you want to append. Otherwise skip this step.

❷ Choose **Append Window** or **Append Selection** from the **File** menu. This opens a directory dialog box.

❸ Select the receiving file (see Chapter R2). The receiving file cannot be open in an Input window.

If you selected an area to append, a dialog box queries whether you want to append only the selected area:

- **Yes** appends only the selected area from the active window.
- **No** appends everything from the active window.
- **Cancel** cancels the append operation.

R3.7 Copying Text

To copy text:

❶ Select the text you want to copy by dragging.

❷ Choose **Copy** from the **Edit** menu. The text is placed on the Clipboard. (As an alternative to choosing **Copy** from the menu, press Command-C.)

❸ Position the insertion point where you want to copy the text. The position does not have to be in the same window from which you copied the text. For example, the original text can be in the Input window, and the position to which you want to copy it can be in the Output window.

❹ Choose **Paste** from the **Edit** menu. As an alternative to choosing **Paste** from the menu, press Command-V. This copies the text into the file. It is also still on the Clipboard.

Lines do not wrap automatically when you copy text. Thus, if the text you are copying would cause the current line to exceed 255 characters, SPSS beeps and does not copy the text.

R3.8 Deleting Text

You can delete individual characters or a block of text. To delete a character:

❶ Position the insertion point after the character and press Delete.

To delete a block of text:

❶ Select the text you want to delete by dragging.

❷ Choose **Clear** from the **Edit** menu. (As an alternative to using the menu, press Delete to delete the highlighted text.)

R3.9 Joining Lines

To join the current line with the previous line:

❶ Position the insertion point at the beginning of the current line.

❷ Press Delete to join the current line to the previous line.

R3.10 Moving Text

To move text:

❶ Drag to select the text you want to move.

❷ Choose **Cut** from the **Edit** menu. As an alternative to using the menu, press Command-X. The text is moved to the Clipboard.

❸ Position the insertion point where you want to move the text. The position does not have to be in the same window from which you cut it. For example, the original text can be in the Input window, and the position to which you want to move it can be in the Output window.

❹ Choose **Paste** from the **File** menu. (As an alternative to using the menu, press Command-V.) This places a copy of the text in place, in the same format as the rest of the window. The text is also still available on the Clipboard.

Lines do not wrap automatically when you move text. Thus, if the text you are moving would cause the current line to exceed 255 characters, SPSS beeps and does not move the text.

R3.11 Pasting Definitions from the Glossary Window

To paste a glossary definition into the active window:

❶ Position the insertion point at the point where you want to paste the definition.

❷ Choose **Glossary Window** from the **Window** menu. This opens the Glossary window.

❸ Type the term in the **Search Entry** box. A definition appears.

❹ Click **Paste.**

The entire definition is pasted into the active window, beginning on the line below the insertion point.

R3.12 Rounding Off Numbers

To round numbers:

❶ To select the numbers you want to round off, drag across one or more lines or hold down Option while you drag diagonally across a rectangle.

❷ Choose **Round** from the **Edit** menu. This opens the **Round Numbers** dialog box, which lets you specify the number of decimal places for rounding or truncation.

❸ Enter the number of decimal positions. The initial default is 0 decimal places. Once you specify a number of decimal places, the specified number becomes the default for the next use.

❹ Click **Round** or **Truncate.**

R3.13 Splitting Lines

To split a line:

❶ Position the insertion point before the character that you want to be the first character on the new line.

❷ Press Return.

R3.14 Typing Characters

The text you type is inserted after the character to the left of the current insertion point; the text to the right of the insertion point moves to make room for the new text.

R3.15 SELECTING TEXT

To select text, you can use the

- **Edit** menu.
- Mouse.

The menu method lets you select complete commands in the Input window and full lines of text in the Output window. With the mouse you can select any string of characters or a rectangular area.

R3.16 Selecting with the Edit Menu

The **Edit** menu provides three options for selecting text. These options vary slightly, depending on whether the Input window or the Output window is active.

R3.17 Selecting Commands

To select commands in the Input window, make the Input window active and then use any of the following options from the **Edit** menu:

- **Select Command** selects the command containing the insertion point, even if some lines of the command are above the insertion point line.
- **Select Current to End** selects multiple commands, beginning with the command containing the insertion point (even if some lines of the command are above the insertion point line) and ending with the last command in the Input window.
- **Select All** selects all text in the Input window.

To find the beginning of a command, SPSS searches up in the Input window from the insertion point until it finds a period at the end of a line. It then uses the line below the period as the first line of the current command. If the period is missing on the previous command, SPSS will select the previous command with the current command and generate an error message. You should check the selected area to be sure you select only the commands you want.

R3.18 Selecting Output Lines

To select lines in the Output window, make the Output window active and then use any of the following options from the **Edit** menu:

- **Select Current to End** selects multiple lines, beginning at the current insertion point line and ending with the last line in the Output window.
- **Select All** selects all lines in the Output window.

R3.19 Selecting with the Mouse

You can use the mouse to

- Select lines in the active window.
- Select a rectangular area in the active window.

You can then use options **Cut, Copy, Paste,** and **Round** on the text in the selected area.

R3.20 Selecting Lines

To use the mouse to select lines, place the insertion point at the beginning of a line and drag the mouse vertically. You can drag the mouse up or down. If you drag the mouse against the top or bottom line visible in the window, lines scroll automatically, as long as you keep the button depressed. If the lines scroll too far, stop scrolling by dragging the mouse back.

When you reach the last line you want to select, move the pointer to the right of the last character you want to select and release the mouse button.

Note: If you have selected the wrong lines, release the mouse button, then click it again. This deselects the area, and you can start over.

To select part of a line, drag horizontally over the text and release the mouse button where you want the selection to end.

R3.21 Selecting a Rectangular Area

To select a rectangular area, press the Option key and drag across and down the area.

R3.22 Deselecting Text

To deselect text, do any of the following:

- Select another area.
- Click anywhere within the window that contains the selected area. The window must be active. If you click in another window, the text from the previous window remains selected.
- Run the commands in the selected area (available only in the Input window).

Chapter R4

Exceptions to the SPSS Reference Guide

This chapter describes SPSS commands or subcommands that differ from the commands described in the *SPSS Reference Guide*.

R4.1 SET SUBCOMMANDS WITH EXCEPTIONS

The SET subcommands that control the contents of the output have exceptions to the way they are documented in the *SPSS Reference Guide*.

- The ERRORS, PRINTBACK, MESSAGES, and RESULTS subcommands on the Macintosh all have options YES or NO, rather than the options given in the *SPSS Reference Guide*. The default is YES for each of these subcommands, meaning that the output contents will include error messages, command printback, resource utilization messages, and results of running SPSS commands. If, for example, you turn off messages by running the command SET MESSAGES NO, you will not see resource utilization messages (how many bytes, etc.) in the output.

- In subcommands that specify characters, such as BOX, the default specification takes advantage of the special characters available on the Macintosh; the characters are not the same as those shown in the *SPSS Reference Guide*. You can run a SHOW BOX command to see the defaults for the Macintosh.

R4.2 ADDITIONAL SET SUBCOMMANDS

One subcommand has been added to SET in the Macintosh version of SPSS. DIRECTORY sets the folder from which all files named on SPSS commands are read and written if the specification does not include a full pathname. This subcommand is equivalent to the **Set Directory** command on the **File** menu. For a full discussion, see Chapter R2.

R4.3 SET SUBCOMMANDS NOT AVAILABLE

Sections R4.4 through R4.5 list SET subcommands that are not available in SPSS for the Macintosh.

R4.4 GRAPH Settings

SPSS for the Macintosh uses the CRICKET command for drawing graphs in Cricket Graph. The CRICKET command is explained in Appendix C. Because the SPSS GRAPH command is not available in SPSS for the Macintosh, the following SET subcommands, which apply to the GRAPH command, are also not available:

- ADEVICE
- DRAW
- GCMDFILE
- GDATA
- GDEVICE
- GMEMORY

R4.5 Other Subcommands Not Available

Several SET subcommands are not applicable to SPSS for the Macintosh either because they cannot be changed or because they are irrelevant. The subcommands TB2, MXWARNS, MXERRS, and XSORT are ignored by SPSS for the Macintosh. The JOURNAL and ENDCMD subcommands do not apply to SPSS for the Macintosh and generate error messages.

R4.6 GET AND SAVE TRANSLATE KEYWORDS

In SPSS for the Macintosh, the TYPE subcommand on the GET TRANSLATE and SAVE TRANSLATE commands has only two keywords.

Specifications for the TYPE subcommand are:

SLK   *Excel or Multiplan SYLK file (symbolic format only).*
TAB   *Tab-delimited file.*

In addition, the TYPE subcommand is required. See Chapter R2 for more information.

R4.7 READ ME FILE VERSUS INFO COMMAND

The SPSS INFO command is not part of SPSS for the Macintosh. For the latest information about SPSS for the Macintosh (that may not be included in any of the printed documentation), open and read the Read Me file on your Setup disk.

Appendix A

Installation and Setup

To install SPSS for the Macintosh you use the Setup program on the SPSS disk labeled **Setup.** During installation, Setup installs all the files *required* to run SPSS for the Macintosh. However, to save disk space, Setup installs a minimum number of optional files used to run SPSS facilities and statistical procedures. It then lets you install more optional modules, or remove some of the optional modules that have been installed.

Any time after the initial installation, you can run Setup to install or remove optional SPSS modules. If you purchase new versions of SPSS for the Macintosh or any of its add-on options, you can run Setup to update files that have already been installed.

Machine Requirements. To install and run SPSS for the Macintosh, you need the following:

- A Mac Plus, a Mac SE, or a Mac II.
- 2MB of memory. If you expect to run SPSS and other applications concurrently under MultiFinder, you need 4MB of memory.
- A hard drive.
- Mac System version 6.0 or higher.
- A minimum of 6MB (6,000K) of available disk space. If you install all of the SPSS for the Macintosh facilities, you will need approximately 15MB (15,000K) of available disk space. (You can find your available disk space by looking in the upper right corner of the disk window, just below the title bar. If it's not there, choose **icon** from the **View** menu.) SPSS also needs some disk space for temporary files.

A.1 INSTALLING SPSS FOR THE MACINTOSH

These instructions assume you are familiar with Macintosh concepts.

❶ Start by opening the window for your hard disk. Be sure the system was started with the system disk or hard disk you intend to use with SPSS.

❷ Insert the **SPSS Setup** disk into a 3.5-inch disk drive. The disk icon appears on the desktop.

❸ Drag the Setup disk icon onto the hard disk icon or into the hard disk window. A dialog box tells you the disks are different types and the files will be placed in a folder on your hard disk.

❹ Click the **OK** button in the dialog box.

A folder named **SPSS 4.0** appears in the hard disk window. (The number may be higher if you have a later version.) The Setup program will put all SPSS files in this folder.

❺ Click the **SPSS 4.0** folder to select it and choose **Open** from the **File** menu (or double-click the **SPSS 4.0** folder). A window for **SPSS 4.0** appears, including icons for SPSS Setup and SPSS Options, a folder for Modules, a Read Me document, TeachText, and folders for the tutorials in this book.

❻ Double-click the Read Me icon to see information that became available after the manuals for SPSS for the Macintosh went to press.

To start the installation process, select the SPSS Setup icon and choose **Open** from the **File** menu or double-click the icon. A dialog box opens, which says **The minimum set of SPSS files is not completely installed** and asks whether to proceed with the installation.

❼ Click the **Yes** button. SPSS Setup ejects the Setup disk and asks for the SPSS utilities disk, **SPSS 4.0 U1.**

❽ Insert the U1 disk.

After you insert the disk, the files are copied. You can watch the progress as the horizontal bar fills up. To stop the installation at any time, click the **Cancel** button. As the Setup program finishes copying the files from one disk, it ejects the disk and asks for another. The installation takes several minutes, and a total of four disks are copied.

The next dialog box appears only if your system is set for fewer than 20 open files at a time. By default the Macintosh system allows 10 open files. Running SPSS requires that the system allow at least 20 files, and probably more, open at a time. We recommend at least 50.

❾ Type 50 and click **OK**. If you change this number, you must restart your computer before using SPSS, as in Step 14. This number can be changed later by choosing **# Open Files** from the **File** menu in the SPSS Setup program.

A dialog box informs you that the SPSS Universal Set is installed. You now have a minimal version of SPSS for the Macintosh on your computer and can proceed with installing additional modules.

⑩ Click the **OK** button. The SPSS Installation window appears, as shown in Figure A.1a. It has two areas: The upper area contains Uninstalled Modules and the lower area contains the Installed Modules.

Figure A.1a *The SPSS Installation window*

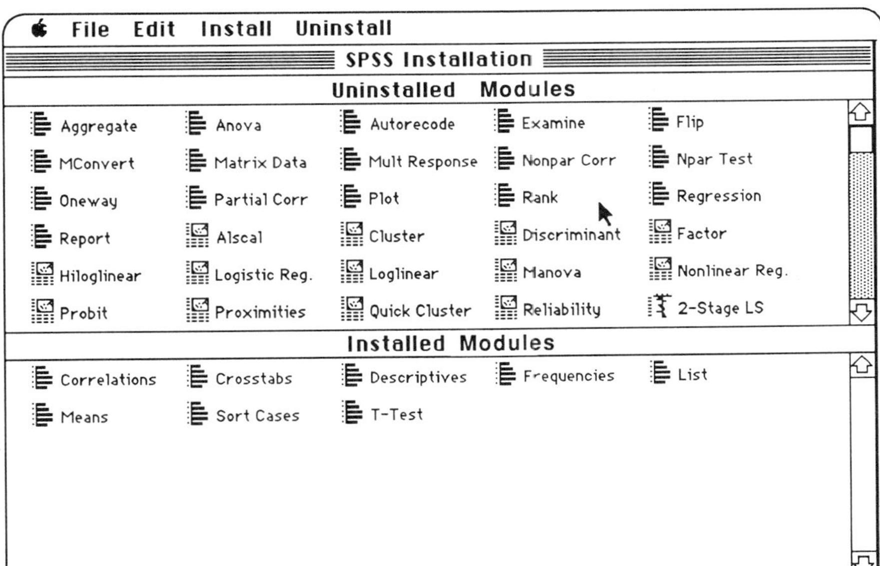

The list of modules that are not installed includes modules from the base system, as well as modules from add-on options (Advanced Statistics, Trends, Tables, and Categories) that you may not have purchased. The group of modules in the base system and in each option are identified by a unique icon.

⑪ Look at the SPSS Installation window to see which modules are installed. If you have as many modules as you need for your work, go to Step 13. Otherwise proceed to Step 12.

A.2   Installing Additional Files

The following instructions assume you are installing the base system and want to select several additional modules. To install the entire base system or an entire add-on option, follow the instructions below in Section A.10. Then return to Step 11.

⑫ Select the additional modules you want to install (you can always use SPSS Setup later to install modules you do not install now). Choose **Selected Options** from the **Install** menu. The Setup program asks for the disks it needs.

⑬ When you have installed all the modules you want, choose **Quit** from the **File** menu. Your SPSS 4.0 folder now contains two applications, several documents, and folders named Modules, Bank, and Value. Inside the Modules folder are all of the modules that were in the lower part of the SPSS Installation window. The Bank and Value folders contain data files and command files for the tutorial chapters in this book.

⑭ If you changed the maximum number of open files, you must restart your computer before running SPSS for the Macintosh. To restart your computer choose **Restart** from the **Special** menu on the Macintosh desktop. The computer ejects any disks left in the 3.5-inch drive before starting up again from the hard disk.

A.3 Online Help

To get online help for the Installation window, click the **Help** button on the **About SPSS** box available from the **Apple** menu, or press Command-H or Command-? You can scroll through the Help topics. You can also access the installation help system by pressing the Help key, if you have one.

A.4 Removing Installed Modules

To remove installed modules, follow the instructions below in Section A.8. Then return to Step 11.

A.5 Preparing Other System Disks

If you plan to start the Macintosh with another system disk and then use SPSS, you must first run the SPSS Setup program on that disk. To prepare the disk:

❶ Use the system disk to start the Macintosh.

❷ Open **SPSS 4.0** on the hard disk drive.

❸ Open **Setup.** If the number of files that can be open is fewer than 20, a dialog box appears to change it. You can also use **# Open Files** on the **File** menu to change the number. The SPSSfont is placed on the system disk.

❹ Choose **Quit** from the **File** menu.

❺ Restart the Macintosh.

A.6 What Next?

You are now done with the Setup program and can begin an SPSS session. To learn the system by following a tutorial during a session, go to Chapter 1. If you prefer to explore SPSS for the Macintosh on your own, Chapter R2 tells you how to begin and quit an SPSS session.

A.7 USING SETUP AFTER SPSS HAS BEEN INSTALLED

At any time after SPSS for the Macintosh has been installed you can use the Setup program to

- Install additional modules that you removed or did not install in earlier runs of Setup.
- Remove modules you do not need.
- Update modules when you purchase new versions of SPSS for the Macintosh software.

A.8 Installing or Removing Optional Files

To install SPSS program files, you must have your SPSS program disks available.
Note: Do not try to install modules by dragging them directly into the Modules folder. The modules on the program disks are compressed and need to be decompressed by running the Setup application.

A.9 Starting Setup

To start Setup on the hard disk:

❶ Double-click the **SPSS 4.0** folder in the hard disk window on the desktop.

❷ Double-click **SPSS Setup** (you may have to scroll to find it).

Setup displays uninstalled modules in the upper area on your screen and installed modules in the bottom area.

A.10 Installing Files That Were Not Previously Installed

You can install

- A set of individual modules.

- All modules from the base system, or all modules from one of the add-on options.
- All modules from the base system, plus all modules from each of the add-on options.

Installing a Set of Individual Modules.   To install a set of individual modules

❶ Select the modules by holding down the Shift key and clicking each icon. You can also drag a rectangle across the modules you want.

❷ Choose **Selected Options** from the **Install** menu.

❸ Each time you are prompted by Setup, insert the appropriate SPSS program disk into the disk drive.

Installing All Files from the Base or a Single Option.   You can easily install all the currently uninstalled modules from the base system or an option (Advanced Statistics, Trends, Tables, or Categories):

❶ Choose the option you want to install from the **Install** menu. Each option is available if any of its modules are not yet installed. For example, if you stopped initially at the minimum number of installed modules, the option Basic Statistics is still available, indicated by boldface type on the menu. If all the modules included in an option have already been installed, that option is dimmed.

❷ Each time you are prompted by Setup, insert the appropriate SPSS program disk into the disk drive.

Installing All Files from All Options.   If you have purchased the base and all of the options (Advanced Statistics, Trends, Tables, and Categories) and you have enough disk space (16MB), you can easily install all the modules from all the options:

❶ Choose **Install All** from the **Install** menu.

❷ Each time you are prompted by Setup, insert the appropriate SPSS program disk into the disk drive.

A.11 Installing SPSSfont

If you want to install the SPSSfont (used for output display) in the Macintosh system so that it will be on menus for Keycaps and othe programs, use the Font/DA Mover. This will allow you to edit text using this font. The Font/DA Mover is described in your Macintosh documentation.

A.12 Removing Installed Files

To remove installed modules with the Setup program:

❶ Select a set of modules by holding down the Shift key and clicking on each module you want to remove.

❷ Choose **Selected Options** from the **Uninstall** menu. The icons of the selected modules move from the Installed Modules section up to Uninstalled Modules, in order by option and alphabetically within the option.

Another way to remove modules is to put them in the Trash can on the Macintosh desktop. From the Finder:

❶ Open the **Modules** folder within the **SPSS 4.0** folder.

❷ Select the set of modules you want to remove by clicking each icon while holding down the Shift key.

❸ Drag the set of modules to the Trash can.

❹ Empty the Trash can by selecting **Empty Trash** from the **Special** menu.

A.13 Updating Installed Files

Updating a file is similar to installing it. When Setup *installs* files, it does not check version numbers. It always replaces the file that is on the computer with the file that is on the disk in the source drive. When Setup *updates* a file, it checks version numbers for the files you want to update. If your computer already has the most current version, Setup leaves it there. If the disk in the source drive has the most current version, Setup installs it. If you are installing modules not previously installed, be sure to use the most recent disk.

The steps for update are:

❶ Choose **Install Update** from the **File** menu. The Setup program asks for the first disk of the update.

❷ Insert other disks as the Setup program asks for them.

❸ If you are updating more than one option—for example, Trends and Advanced Statistics—you must run the update process individually for each option.

Important Macintosh Concepts

This appendix provides information on some Macintosh features you can use with SPSS for the Macintosh. If you are new to the Macintosh, you can find operating information in the *User's Guide* that came with your Macintosh System Software. This appendix highlights some of the features that will help you operate SPSS for the Macintosh efficiently.

B.1 MANIPULATING WINDOWS

As in many Macintosh applications, you can place SPSS windows in convenient positions and change the sizes of many of them. Figure B.1a indicates some of the useful features of a window.

Figure B.1a *SPSS window*

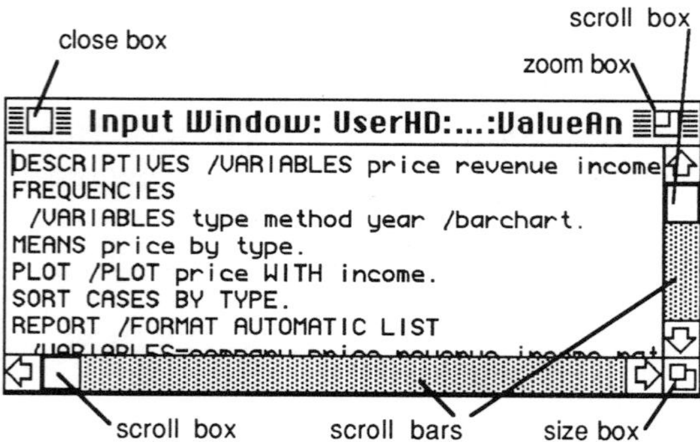

B.2 Closing a Window

To close a window, click the close box in the upper left corner.

B.3 Enlarging a Window

To enlarge a window, use one of the following methods:

- Click the zoom box in the upper right corner. The first time you click the zoom box, the window zooms out to fill the whole screen. If you click the zoom box again, the window zooms back to its previous size.
- Drag the size box. You can drag the size box in the lower right corner until the window is the size you want.

B.4 Moving a Window

To move a window around the screen, move the pointer to the title bar and press and hold the mouse button. Drag the window where you want it; then release the mouse button. For example, you may want to open the Help window or the Glossary window and drag it to the corner of the screen. You can then leave the window open while you work.

B.5 Using the Keyboard to Move the Pointer

If you have the Macintosh file **Easy Access** in your Macintosh System Folder, you can use the Mouse Keys (the numbered keys on the keypad) to move the pointer, as described in the *Macintosh System Software User's Guide*. To set the keypad keys as mouse keys, press Command-Shift-Clear.

B.6 Scrolling a Window

Sometimes a window contains more information than can be seen at one time in the window. To display the hidden information you can scroll the window either horizontally or vertically. Such windows have *horizontal scroll bars* on the bottom and *vertical scroll bars* on the right side of the window. The scroll bar contains arrows at either end and a box in the middle.

To scroll up one line of information, click the up arrow in the vertical scroll bar; to scroll down one line of information, click the down arrow in the vertical scroll bar. To scroll one character to the left, click the left arrow in the horizontal scroll bar; to scroll one character to the right, click the right arrow in the horizontal scroll bar.

To scroll up one page of information, click in the area between the scroll box and the up arrow. To scroll down one page of information, click in the area between the box and the down arrow. To scroll right one screen of information, click in the area between the scroll box and the right arrow. To scroll left one screen of information, click in the area between the box and the left arrow.

You can quickly scroll horizontally or vertically by dragging the appropriate scroll box.

B.7 PRINTING

If you choose a **Print** command, a standard Macintosh print dialog box appears. Its contents depend on the type of printer indicated in your Chooser. Figure B.7a shows a typical print dialog box.

Figure B.7a *Print dialog box*

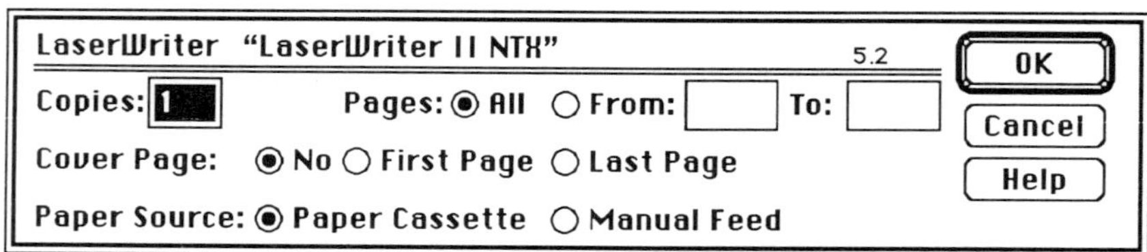

To print the entire contents of a file displayed in a window, or a specified group of pages, choose **Print Window** from the **File** menu. In the dialog box you can indicate how many copies you want and which pages to print. You can also indicate whether you want a cover page and whether the paper is fed automatically or manually.

If you want to print a selected area of the window, select an area of text and then choose **Print Selection** from the **File** menu. In this case, leave the **Pages** radio button with **All** selected (the default). If you use an ImageWriter, select **Best** or **Faster** quality. **Draft** is not compatible with SPSSfont.

B.8 Choosing Printing Features

The **Page Setup** command on the **File** menu lets you choose several printing features, such as whether you want portrait or landscape orientation. These features are displayed in a standard Macintosh dialog box, which is described in the *Macintosh System Software User's Guide*. You can click the **Help** button for brief information on the options. You can often print with the default settings and not use **Page Setup** at all. One setting SPSS users commonly change is to use landscape orientation for a file 132 characters wide.

If you click **Page Setup** when the Output window is active, the page size and orientation you choose will generate and run SPSS SET commands for page length and width. These commands are printed at the bottom of the Output window.

B.9   ACTIVATING A BUTTON

Buttons in a window allow you to initiate functions. There are several ways to activate the button:

- Move the pointer to the button and click.
- Often, you can type the first letter of the name of the button. For example, in the dialog box that asks if you want to save a file before quitting SPSS, typing **N** activates the **No** button and typing **Y** activates the **Yes** button.
- If one of the buttons is displayed with a thicker outline, it is the default button. To activate the default button, you can press the Return key.

B.10   RUNNING COMMANDS WITH THE ENTER KEY

You can run a command or a selected set of SPSS commands by pressing the Enter key. Be sure to press Enter, not Return. Pressing the Return key moves the insertion point to the next line. If the insertion point is in the middle of text, pressing Return splits the line.

B.11   WORKING IN MORE THAN ONE APPLICATION

If you have MultiFinder on, you can work in other applications while SPSS for the Macintosh is processing its commands. For example, suppose you are working with a large data file and have started running an SPSS CROSSTABS command. The status box appears with the message **SPSS working...** and the pointer is a spinning beachball. You can switch to another application such as MacWrite, use it for a while, and then come back to SPSS. If SPSS finishes processing before you return, it sends the results to the Output window and is ready when you switch back.

Drawing Graphs with Cricket Graph

If you have Cricket Graph installed, you can use the SPSS CRICKET command to aggregate or count SPSS data according to a statistical function that you select. Then SPSS writes out a data file in Cricket Graph format.

This appendix is divided into two parts:

- Sections C.1 through C.8 describe how to use Cricket and provide several examples.
- Sections C.9 through C.20 contain the CRICKET command reference.

C.1 RUNNING CRICKET GRAPH

Sections C.2 and C.3 provide a step-by-step example of generating a data file for Cricket and then drawing the graph. Sections C.4 through C.8 contain examples of the CRICKET command used for various types of graphs. The instructions in this section assume you know how to generate and run a simple command in SPSS. For more information on SPSS commands see Chapter 1 and Chapter R2.

C.2 Running a Basic CRICKET Command

The steps below and in Section C.3 show you how to draw a chart in Cricket Graph using the MEAN function and data from the SPSS system file Value.SPSS-Sys, which came with your SPSS system. This example uses the Command Generator.

Assume you want a simple column graph showing average selling prices for the different types of software companies in the data.

❶ Start an SPSS session by double-clicking on the SPSS icon.

❷ Choose **Get SPSS System File** from the **File** menu. This opens a directory dialog box.

❸ Double-click the **Value** folder and select **Value.SPSS-Sys.**

❹ Click the **Get** button. The data and definitions from the Value.SPSS-Sys file are now in the active SPSS system file.

❺ Choose **Set Directory** from the **File** menu and click the **Select this directory** button. Setting the directory tells SPSS to put files named on the OUTFILE subcommand into the Value folder instead of the SPSS 4.0 folder.

❻ Make the Input window active by clicking in it. Then type **cricket.**

❼ Choose **Command Generator** from the **Window** menu. The Command Generator window opens with a list of CRICKET subcommands.

❽ Select **/TABLE** and click **Next.**

❾ Select **summary function** and click **Next.**

❿ Select **MEAN** from the list and paste it.

⓫ Click **Prev.**

⓬ Select and paste the parentheses ().

⓭ Select **variables** and click **Paste** to open the Variables window.

⓮ Select **PRICE** and click **Paste.**

⓯ Go back to the **TABLE** menu.

⓰ Select **BY** and **variables**, and paste variable **TYPE.**

⓱ Go back to the CRICKET menu of subcommands, paste the subcommand **/OUTFILE** and type the filename **Price.Cricket.** The Command Generator supplies the apostrophes. Without apostrophes, the filename will be all lower case. Be sure there is a period is at the end of the command.

⓲ Click **Run & Close.** This creates a file Price.Cricket in your Value folder.

C.3 Draw a Graph

To draw the graph from the new file, start at the desktop.

❶ Open the **Value** folder and double-click the Price.Cricket icon.

❷ Choose **Column** from the **Graph** menu. A dialog box opens.

❸ Select **Type of Software** in the categories list and **Mean Price** in the values list.

❹ Click the **New Plot** button. The column graph appears, as shown in Figure C.3a.

Figure C.3a *Column graph*

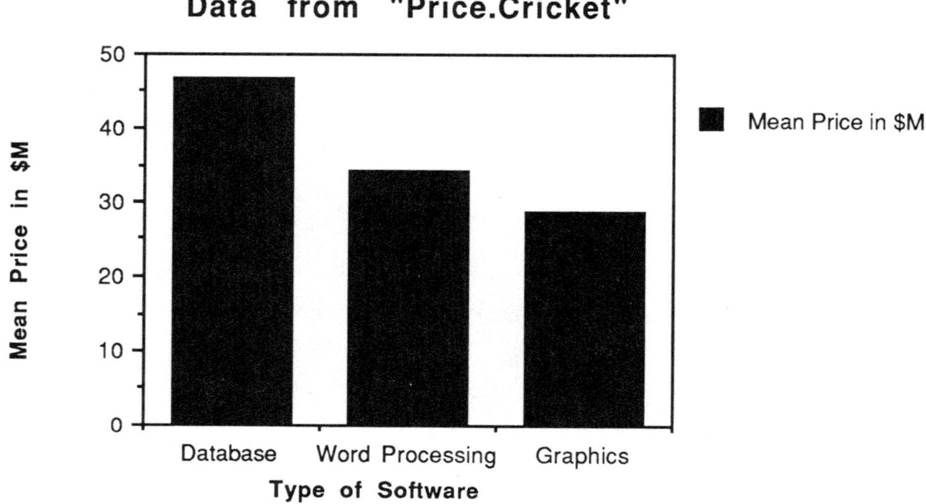

You can adjust any elements of the graph, following the instructions in the Cricket Graph documentation. For example, to change the axis label Mean Price to Average Price, double-click on the vertical-axis label.

C.4 Examples

Several examples of CRICKET commands are included in the file Cricket.Templates in your Bank folder. They are also listed here and discussed. Before running the following CRICKET commands, choose **Get SPSS System File** from the **File** menu and select the file **Bank.SPSS-Sys** from the **Bank** folder.

You can use these examples in several ways:

- Practice generating CRICKET commands with the Command Generator.
- Run several of the CRICKET commands in Cricket.Templates, starting with the data in Bank.SPSS-Sys or Value.SPSS-Sys.

- Open the resulting data files in Cricket Graph and draw the graphs. You can open several files at once and experiment with graph types and formats.
- Copy a CRICKET command from the Cricket.Templates file to a new SPSS Input window and modify it to use the variables in one of your own data files. Get your data file, run the CRICKET command, and then draw the graph in Cricket Graph.

C.5 Line Graph

The file generated by the following command can be used to draw a simple line graph. If you include more variables in the variable list in parentheses, you can draw several lines in the same graph. The variables should be measured in the same units.

```
CRICKET /TABLE=MEAN(SALNOW) BY EDLEVEL
   /OUTFILE=SalaryEdlevel.Cricket.
```

In Cricket Graph, choose **Line** from the **Graph** menu. Then select **EDUCATIONAL LEVEL** as the horizontal axis and **Mean CURRENT SALARY** as the vertical axis. If you choose **Hide Legend** from the **Goodies** menu, the graph looks like Figure C.5a.

Figure C.5a *Line graph*

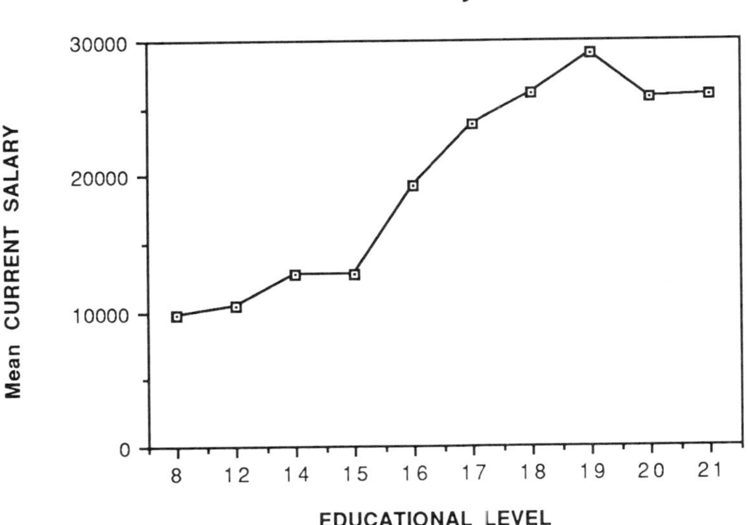

Changing the Scale.   To change the scale, you first need to convert the data format to numeric:

❶ Make the data window active and select the first column.

❷ Choose **Column Format** from the **Data** menu. The format is alphabetical, because EDLEVEL was the variable after BY in the CRICKET command.

❸ Click the **Decimal** radio button and then the **OK** button. A dialog box about data being converted appears.

❹ Click **OK**.

❺ Choose **Line** from the **Graph** menu again, and click **New Plot**. A new graph appears, on which you can change the scales because the data are now numeric.

❻ Double-click the horizontal axis and change the values to Minimum 8, Maximum 22, and Increment 2.

The result is shown in Figure C.5b.

Figure C.5b *Line graph with numeric scale*

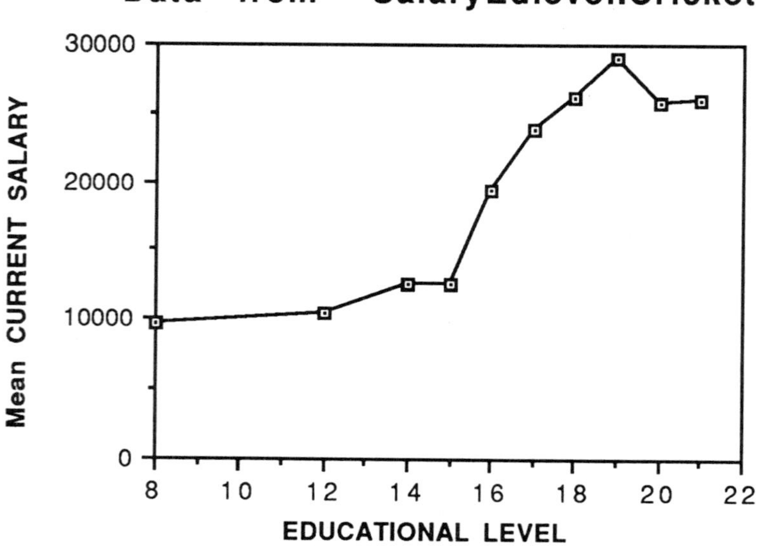

C.6 Pie Chart

The data generated by the following command can be used to draw a pie chart, illustrating the relationship of each job category to the total number of jobs.

```
CRICKET /TABLE=COUNT BY JOBCAT
 /OUTFILE='JobCategories.Cricket'.
```

In Cricket Graph choose **Pie** from the **Graph** menu. Select **EMPLOYMENT CATEGORIES** as the category and **Count** as the value. You can drag one of the sections out of the pie if you want to. (For some printers you may need to check the **Tall Adjusted** box on **Page Setup** from the **File** menu. This produces better circles.) Figure C.6a shows the pie chart.

Figure C.6a *Pie chart*

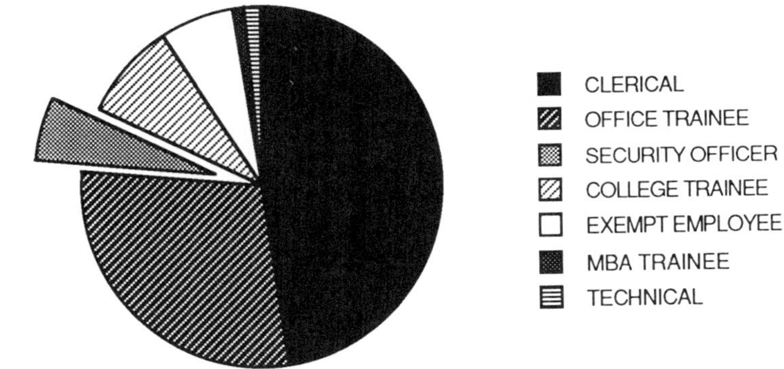

C.7 Scatterplots

The data from the following command can be used to explore the relationship between current salary and beginning salary. If you include more than two variables, the category values are each represented by a different symbol.

```
CRICKET /CASEFILE=SALBEG SALNOW
 /OUTFILE='Salaries.Cricket'.
```

In Cricket Graph choose **Scatter** from the **Graph** menu and then choose
BEGINNING SALARY for the horizontal axis and **CURRENT SALARY** for
the vertical axis. Figure C.7a shows the scatterplot.

Figure C.7a *Scatterplot*

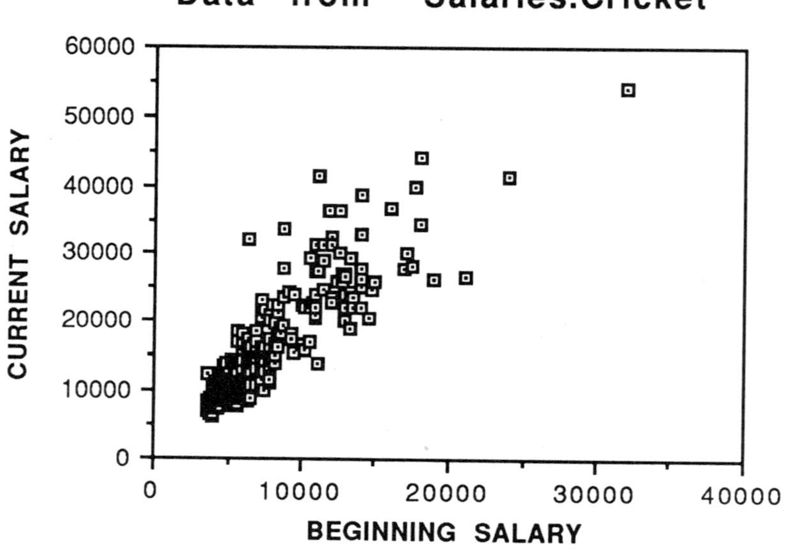

The data for a scatterplot can be divided into categories. For example, the
following command divides the beginning and current salaries by job category:

```
CRICKET /CASEFILE=SALBEG SALNOW BY JOBCAT
 /OUTFILE='SalByJob.Cricket'.
```

The data file has many empty cells, as shown in Figure C.7b.

To produce the graph, choose **Scatter** from the **Graph** menu. Select
BEGINNING SALARY for the horizontal axis and **CURRENT SALARY** for
SECURITY OFFICER, EXEMPT EMPLOYEE, and **MBA TRAINEE** for
the vertical axis. As shown in Figure C.7c, each category has a different
symbol. The vertical axis takes the name of the first category. Double-click the
label of the vertical axis and change it to **CURRENT SALARY.** You can also
change the symbols by double-clicking on the legend.

Figure C.7b *Casefile data*

	1 BEGINNING SALARY	2 CURRENT SALARY CLERICAL	3 CURRENT SALARY OFF
1	84000		
2	24000		
3	10200		
4	8700		
5	17400		
6	12996		
7	6900	16080	
8	5400	14100	
9	5040	12420	
10	6300		
11	6300	15720	
12	6000	8880	
13	10500		
14	10800		
15	13200		

Figure C.7c *Scatterplot with categories*

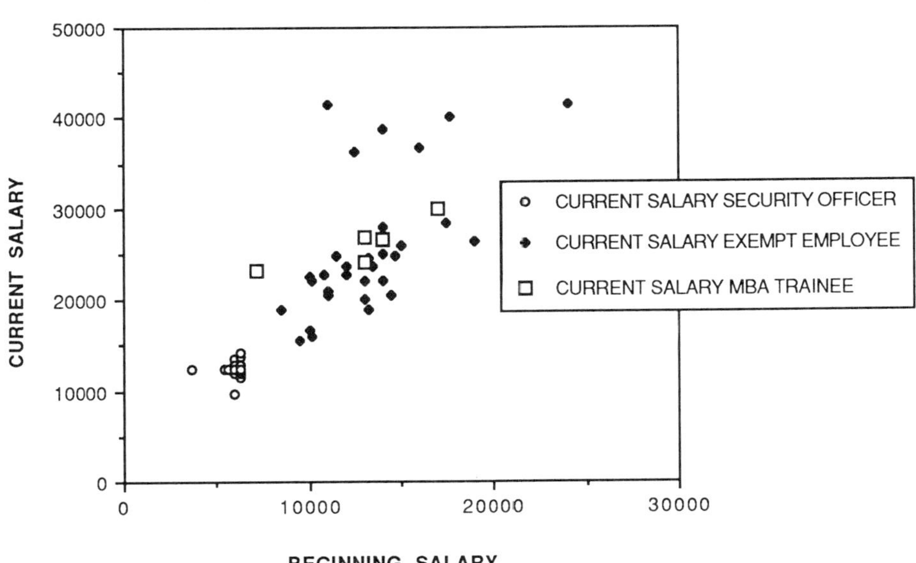

C.8 Histogram

In the following command the data are divided into bins so that you can draw
a histogram showing the number in each bin:

```
CRICKET /TABLE=BIN BY SALNOW
 /OUTFILE='SalaryBins.Cricket'.
```

In Cricket Graph, choose **Bar** or **Column** from the **Graph** menu and select
CURRENT SALARY as the category and **Count** as the value. The scale will
indicate the midpoint of each bin.

C.9 CRICKET COMMAND REFERENCE

Sections C.10 through C.20 include syntax and complete information on all of
the subcommands for CRICKET.

C.10 Syntax

```
CRICKET
  {/TABLE={sumf(varlist) [BY cvar]          }}
  {         {sumf(sumvar) BY cvar [BY cvar ]}}
  {         {countf BY var [BY cvar ]       }}
  {         {[COUNT BY] var                 }}
  {/CASEFILE= varlist [BY var]              }

   /OUTFILE=filename
```

where

var=	variable
varlist=	list of variables
sumvar=	summary variable
cvar=	category variable
sumf=	summary function
countf=	count function

Summary functions (sumf):

MINIMUM	Minimum
MAXIMUM	Maximum
N	Weighted N
SUM	Sum
CUSUM	Cumulative sum
MEAN	Mean
STDDEV	Standard deviation
VARIANCE	Variance
MEDIAN	Median
MODE	Mode
PTILE(x)	Xth percentile
PLT(x)	Percent less than x
PGT(x)	Percent greater than x
NLT(x)	Number less than x
NGT(x)	Number greater than x
PIN(x1,x2)	Percent between x1 and x2
NIN(x1,x2)	Number between x1 and x2

Count functions (countf):

COUNT	Count
PCT	Percent
CUPCT	Cumulative percent
FREQ	Frequency
CUFREQ	Cumulative frequency
BIN	Bins for histogram

C.11 Overview

The CRICKET command aggregates or counts data for producing a chart in Cricket Graph. You can use the data to draw any type of chart available in Cricket Graph, including, but not limited to, bar, pie, line, and area graphs, and scatterplots. You can also generate data for histograms.

Data.   The TABLE subcommand provides functions for aggregating or counting the data in your SPSS file. You can also transfer actual SPSS data to Cricket Graph format by using the CASEFILE subcommand.

Output File.   You must specify a file to which SPSS for the Macintosh sends the data.

Launching Cricket Graph.   After the data file is written, you can launch Cricket Graph to draw the graph. Both SPSS for the Macintosh and Cricket Graph work with MultiFinder, if you have enough memory. If you are operating with the Finder, you can launch Cricket Graph after leaving SPSS.

Multiple Files.   You can run several CRICKET commands in SPSS for the Macintosh and later access all the files in single Cricket Graph session.

C.12 Subcommand Order

Subcommands can be named in any order.

C.13 Syntax Rules

- Only one TABLE or CASEFILE subcommand can be specified per CRICKET command.
- The OUTFILE subcommand is required.

C.14 Operations

- You must have Cricket Graph on your system to draw the graphs from the CRICKET command.
- The CRICKET command creates a data file in Cricket Graph format. The data file can be opened in Cricket Graph.
- If you double-click the file icon on the desktop, Cricket Graph opens and loads the SPSS data.
- You can create a CRICKET command by using the SPSS Command Generator or by typing the command in the SPSS Input window.
- If a value label exists for a value, that value is included in the file built by the CRICKET command and is included in most types of charts even if that value is defined as missing or if no cases with that value occur in the data. You can select categories for the graph from the columns in the Cricket Graph data file.
- Variable labels for non-aggregated variables are passed to Cricket Graph and used as column labels.
- For aggregated variables, labels are constructed from the summary function name and the variable label. For instance, STDDEV(SALBET) would have the label **Stddev BEGINNING SALARY.** You can easily modify a label in Cricket Graph by double-clicking and then editing the name, font, and style.

C.15 Limitations

- Up to 100 variables can be aggregated with CRICKET.
- Summary function: 100 variables.
- Summary function BY cvar BY cvar: 99 values for the second cvar.
- Count function BY cvar: 99 values for the cvar.
- Variable list: 100 variables.
- Variable list BY var: the sum of the number of variables in the variable list plus the number of values (distinct categories) in the last variable must be less than 100.
- Maximum length of a column label in Cricket Graph is 31 characters. Longer labels will be truncated.

C.16 Examples

```
CRICKET /TABLE=SUM(MURDER) BY CITY
 /OUTFILE = 'MurdersCity.Cricket'.
```

- The TABLE subcommand specifies a summary function with one summary variable and a category variable.
- The OUTFILE subcommand specifies the filename.

```
CRICKET /TABLE=MEAN (AGE) BY EYECOLOR
 /OUTFILE='MeanAge.Cricket'.
```

- The TABLE subcommand creates an aggregated SPSS system file from which it generates a tab-delimited data file containing the summary variable MEAN AGE and the category variable EYE COLOR. The data could be used to create any kind of chart that can be made with a single summary variable and a single category variable. In Cricket Graph, select **Eyecolor** as the category and **Mean Age** as the value.

C.17 TABLE Subcommand

The TABLE subcommand specifies one summary or count function, one or more variables to summarize, and one or more variables that determine the groups within which the function is calculated. CRICKET assumes the category value is alphabetical (string) unless you change it using **Column Format** from the **Data** menu.

Examples.   The following subcommand specifies a summary function with one category variable:

```
/TABLE = MEAN(SALES REVENUE) BY MONTH
```

The following subcommand specifies a summary function with two category variables:

```
/TABLE = MEAN(SALARY) BY JOBCAT BY DEPT
```

The following subcommand specifies a count function:

```
/TABLE = COUNT BY JOBCAT
```

C.18 Histograms

Subcommand TABLE with the count function BIN generates data files suitable for histograms. SPSS determines the sizes of bins based on the sample size.

```
CRICKET /TABLE=BIN BY SALBEG
  /OUTFILE='BeginSalary.Cricket'.
```

In Cricket Graph, choose **Bar** or **Column** from the **Graph** menu.

C.19 TABLE Functions

Two types of functions are available: *summary functions* and *count functions*. In the Command Generator, these functions are all in one list.

Summary Functions.   These functions are usually used with variables that record continuous values, like age or expenses. To specify a summary function, put the name of one or more variables in parentheses after the name of the function, as in:

```
/TABLE=SUM(SALARY) BY DEPT
```

If the summary function listed below shows x, x1, or x2 in parentheses, replace each with a numeric value, as in:

```
/TABLE=PTILE(75)(SALARY) BY DEPT
```

The following summary functions are available:

MINIMUM	*Minimum value of the variable.*
MAXIMUM	*Maximum value of the variable.*
N	*Number of cases for which the variable has a non-missing value.*
SUM	*Sum of the values of the variable.*
CUSUM	*Sum of the summary variable, accumulated across values of the category variable.*

MEAN	*Mean.*
STDDEV	*Standard deviation.*
VARIANCE	*Variance.*
MEDIAN	*Median.*
MODE	*Mode.*
PTILE(x)	*Xth percentile value of the variable.* x must be greater than 0 and less than 100.
PLT(x)	*Percentage of cases for which the variable is less than x.*
PGT(x)	*Percentage greater than x.*
NLT(x)	*Number less than x.*
NGT(x)	*Number greater than x.*
PIN(x1,x2)	*Percentage of cases for which the variable is greater than or equal to x1, and less than or equal to x2.* x1 must be no greater than x2.
NIN(x1,x2)	*Number of cases for which the variable is greater than or equal to x1, and less than or equal to x2.* x1 must be no greater than x2.

Count Functions.   Count functions yield the count or percentage of valid cases with categories determined by one or more BY variables, as in:

```
/TABLE=PCT BY REGION
```

In places where COUNT BY *variable* is expected, you can specify just a variable, as in

```
/TABLE=DEPT
```

This is interpreted as COUNT BY DEPT, even though the function COUNT and the keyword BY are not explicitly specified.

The count functions are as follows:

COUNT	*Count of cases in each category.*
PCT	*Count of cases in each category expressed as a percentage of the whole.*
CUPCT	*Cumulative percentage.*
FREQ	*Frequency.* FREQ is the same as COUNT.
CUFREQ	*Cumulative frequency.*
BIN	*Division of data into intervals for a histogram.* SPSS determines the appropriate number of bins based on the sample size.

C.20 CASEFILE Subcommand

CASEFILE builds a file of unaggregated cases that can be used within Cricket Graph to generate scatterplots and other graphs using actual SPSS data. The data file contains the actual values of each variable listed. You can sample the data or limit them in some other way before running the CRICKET command.

The specification on CASEFILE is simply the variable names, as in:

```
/CASEFILE = SALARY GRADE
```

The Cricket Graph data file contains a column for SALARY and a column for GRADE. Choose one for the vertical axis and one for the horizontal axis. With the subcommand

```
/CASEFILE = SALARY BONUS BY JOBCAT
```

the Cricket Graph data file contains a column for SALARY and columns for BONUS by JOBCAT. The data for categories are scattered in many columns. Even though many cells are empty, the data are all in the table. If you draw a scatterplot with SALARY on the horizontal axis and BONUS for each job category on the vertical axis, each category has a different plot symbol.

Variable Format Types

This appendix defines the variable format types available with SPSS for the Macintosh.

D.1 INPUT AND OUTPUT FORMATS

Table D.1a shows the *input* data formats available in SPSS for the Macintosh. Input formats are the formats SPSS uses when it reads data. Table D.1b shows the *output* data formats available in SPSS for the Macintosh. Output formats are the formats SPSS uses to display output or to write data to other software programs. In both tables, w represents the variable width and d represents the number of decimal places.

When format types are specified with column-style specifications on DATA LIST, the column locations determine the variable width, so you do not specify a width. To include decimal positions in column-style specification, use a comma to separate the format type from the number of decimal positions, as in DOLLAR,2.

- Based on the input formats, SPSS automatically generates output formats. For some formats (for example, A format or F format with freefield data) SPSS generates output formats that are identical to the input formats. For others (for example, DOLLAR or PCT format, or F format with fixed data) SPSS automatically increases the width of the output format to accommodate punctuation. For example, an input format of PCT4.1 specifies a variable with a maximum width of 4. SPSS generates an output format of PCT6.1 to allow for a four-digit number plus one decimal point and one percent sign.

- To change the output formats for a variable, use the FORMATS, PRINT FORMATS, or WRITE FORMATS commands. Formats can also be specified for printed and written output on the PRINT and WRITE commands.

- Decimal positions in the format specification affect the way SPSS displays values in output; they do not affect calculations. For example, assume format F5.0 is specified for both variables v1 and v2, and that both v1 and v2 have the value 100.5. In a case listing, the displayed value for both v1 and v2 is 101, since F5.0 format specifies 0 decimal places and, for display purposes, SPSS rounds off each value to the nearest whole number. If v3 is computed as the sum of v1 and v2, however, v3 nevertheless equals 201 because the display format does not affect calculations.

Implied Decimal Positions. Decimal positions can be *implied* when they are not coded in the data. This can be done only for fixed-format data. Decimal places cannot be implied for freefield data.

- By default, SPSS assumes the data are whole numbers or that decimal points have been recorded on the data file.
- *For fixed data:* If a value has no coded decimal point but the input format specifies decimal positions, the rightmost positions are interpreted as *implied* decimal digits. For example, if the input format specifies 2 decimal digits, the value 1234 is interpreted as 12.34. However, the value 123.4 is interpreted as 123.40.

- *For freefield data:* If a value has no coded decimal point, SPSS reads numbers as whole numbers. Decimal points must be coded in the value if decimal positions are to be read. For example, if the input format specifies 2 decimal digits, the value 1234 is interpreted as 1234.00; the value 123.4 is interpreted as 123.40.

Table D.1a *Input data formats*

Input format	Min w	Max w	Implied d (max)	Input blank	Default output type	Notes
Printable numerics						
Fw.d	1	40	16	SET	same	
Nw	1	40		SET	F	
Nw.d	1	40	16	SET	F	
Ew.d	1	40	15	SET	same	w is the greater of w, d+7, or 10
Ew	1	40		SET	same	w is the greater of w or 10
COMMAw.d	1	40	16	SET	same	
COMMAw	1	40		SET	same	
DOTw.d	1	40	16	SET	same	
DOLLARw.d	1	40	16	SET	same	
DOLLARw	1	40		SET	same	
PCTw.d	1	40	16	SET	same	

Input format	Min w	Max w	Implied d (max)	Input blank	Default output type	Notes
PIBHEXw	2	8		SET	F	w must be an even number
PIBHEXw	2	16		SET	F	w must be an even number
RBHEXw	4	16		SET	F	w must be an even number
Zw.d	1	40	16	SET	F	
Zw	1	40		SET	F	
Nonprintable numerics						
IBw.d	1	8	16	value	F	w is in bytes, d is decimal digits
IBw	1	8		value	F	w is in bytes
PIBw.d	1	8	16	value	F	w is in bytes, d is decimal digits
PIBw	1	8		value	F	w is in bytes
Pw.d	1	16	16	SET	F	
Pw	1	16		SET	F	
PKw.d	1	16	16	value	F	
PKw	1	16		value	F	
RBw	2	8		value	F	w must be an even number
Strings						
Aw	1	255		blank	same	
AHEXw	2	254		blank	A	w must be an even number
Bit						
column:row				SET	F	column binary format
byte:bit				SET	F	UPIB format
Spacing						
Tn	1	n/a*				tabs to column n
nX	1	n/a*				skips n columns
Date and time						**Input form**
DATEw	9	40		SET	same	dd/mmm/yy
ADATEw	8	40		SET	same	mm/dd/yy
JDATEw	5	40		SET	same	yyddd
QYRw	4	40		SET	same	qQyy
MOYRw	6	40		SET	same	mm/yyyy
WKYRw	6	40		SET	same	wkWKyy
TIMEw	5	40		SET	same	hh:mm:ss.ss
DTIMEw	11	40		SET	same	d hh:mm:ss.ss
DATETIMEw	17	40		SET	same	dd/mmm/yy hh:mm:ss.ss
WKDAYw	2	40		SET	same	dd
MONTHw	3	40		SET	same	mmm

*Not applicable

Table D.1b *Output data formats*

Format type	PRINT	Min w	Max w	Max d	Result form
Numeric					
Fw, Fw.d	yes	1*	40	16	
COMMAw, COMMAw.d	yes	1*	40	16	
DOTw, DOTw.d	yes	1*	40	16	
DOLLARw, DOLLARw.d	yes	2*	40	16	
CCw, CCw.d	yes	2*	40	16	
PCTw, PCTw.d	yes	1*	40	16	
PIBHEXw	yes	2**	16**		
RBHEXw	yes	4**	16**		
Zw, Zw.d	yes	1	40	16	
IBw, IBw.d	no	1	8	16	
PIBw, PIBw.d	no	1	8	16	
Nw	yes	1	40		
Pw, Pw.d	no	1	16	16	
Ew, Ew.d	yes	6	40		
PKw, PKw.d	no	1	16	16	
RBw	no	2	8		
String					
Aw	yes	1	254		
AHEXw	yes	2**	510		
Date and time					
DATEw	yes	9	40		dd-mmm-yy
		11			dd-mmm-yyyy
ADATEw	yes	8	40		mm/dd/yy
		10			mm/dd/yyyy
JDATEw	yes	5	40		yyddd
		7			yyyyddd
QYRw	yes	6	40		q Q yy
		8			q Q yyyy
MOYRw	yes	6	40		mmm yy
		8			mmm yyyy
WKYRw	yes	8	40		ww WK yy
		10			ww WK yyyy
WKDAYw	yes	2+	40		
MONTHw	yes	3+	40		
TIMEw	yes	5++	40		hh:mm
TIMEw.d	yes	10	40	16	hh:mm:ss.s
DTIMEw	yes	8++	40		dd hh:mm
DTIMEw.d	yes	13	40	16	dd hh:mm:ss.s
DATETIMEw	yes	17++	40		dd-mmm-yyyy hh:mm
DATETIMEw.d	yes	22	40	16	dd-mmm-yyyy hh:mm:ss.s

*Add number of decimals plus 1 if number of decimals is more than 1. Total width cannot exceed 40 characters.
**Must be a multiple of 2.
+As the field width is expanded, the output string is expanded until the entire name of the day or month is produced.
++Add 3 to display seconds.

D.2 Printable Numeric Formats

Generally, each of the printable numeric formats adhere to the conventions discussed below:

- *For fixed data:* Blank fields read with any of the printable numeric formats are set to system- missing by default or to the value specified on the BLANK subcommand on the SET command.
- *For freefield data:* A blank in the data is interpreted as the end of the value.
- *For fixed data:* Decimal positions can be implied in the format.
- *For freefield data:* Decimal positions cannot be implied.

The following conventions apply to output formats:

- The default print and write formats include enough space for printing and writing punctuation characters (decimal points, commas, dollar signs, etc.).
- Formats specified on PRINT FORMATS, WRITE FORMATS, FORMATS, or in PRINT and WRITE commands must allow enough positions to include any punctuation characters such as decimal points, commas, dollar signs, or date and time delimiters. SPSS *does not* automatically expand the output formats you assign. The column labeled **Max d** in Table D.1b indicates the maximum number of decimal places allowed for each format type.
- If a data value exceeds its width specification, SPSS makes an attempt to produce some value nevertheless. It takes out punctuation characters, then it tries scientific notation, and only then, if there is still not enough space, it produces asterisks indicating that a value is present which cannot be printed in the assigned width.
- By default, SPSS translates restricted numeric, hexadecimal numeric, and zoned input formats to output formats of standard numeric (F). All other printable input formats retain the same output format type (see Table D.1a).

D.3 Fw.d (Standard Numeric)

The F format reads standard numeric values. Each input value can include a maximum of one decimal point. Dollar signs, commas, and percent signs cannot be coded in the data.

For fixed data, if a value has no coded decimal point but the input format specifies decimal positions, the rightmost positions are interpreted as *implied* decimal digits. For example, if the input format specifies 2 decimal digits, the value 1234 is interpreted as 12.34. However, the value 123.4 is still interpreted as 123.4. For freefield data, decimal digits cannot be implied.

The F format accepts numbers in scientific notation, provided the data values include E or D, the sign, and the power of 10. For example, the data value 543E+3 can be read under an F6 format. If a value is coded in scientific notation, an implied decimal specification is ignored.

The default output formats are type F. Thus, assuming there are no implied decimal positions in the input format, the value 1234 is displayed in output as 1234.

D.4 Nw.d (Restricted Numeric)

The N format is used to specify fields containing unsigned integers. Leading, trailing, and imbedded blanks are not allowed. You can specify the number of digits that follow an implied decimal point. Coded decimal values are not allowed. This format is useful for reading and checking values that you know should be only integers with leading zeros.

For example, N2 defines a two-column variable. The value 2 must be entered as 02. Leading blanks are not allowed. A completely blank field is assigned system-missing.

The default output formats are type F.

D.5 Ew.d (Scientific Notation)

The E format reads all forms of scientific notation numbers. As an input format, E format can read an embedded E or D symbol and an embedded + or − sign. If the sign is omitted, + is assumed. If the sign is coded in the data, the E or D can be omitted. In addition, E format can read any value that is acceptable to F format. Thus, assuming the input format E9, the input values 1.234E+03, 1.234E3, 1.234+3, and 1234 are equivalent.

The input value can be up to 40 columns wide, and can include up to 15 decimal positions. For fixed field data, the decimal positions can be implied. For example, assuming an E4.3 input format and keyword FIXED on DATA LIST, the value 1234 is interpreted as 1.234E+00. For freefield data, decimal positions cannot be implied. For example, assuming an E4.3 input format and keyword FREE on DATA LIST, the value 1234 is interpreted as 1.234E+03. Decimal points cannot be coded in the exponent portion of the value.

The default output formats are type E with a minimum width of 10 columns, 3 of which are decimal positions (E10.3). For the output width, SPSS uses either the specified input width, the number of specified decimal positions plus 7 (d+7), or 10, whichever is greater. Thus, the input format E12.4 is unchanged as an output format. The input format E7.4 generates the output format E11.4. The input format E4.3 generates the output format E10.3. If 0, 1, or 2 decimal positions are specified in the input format, SPSS nonetheless uses

3 decimal positions in the output format. Thus, the input format EII.2 generates the output format EII.3.

Output formats assigned on FORMATS, PRINT FORMATS, and WRITE FORMATS are not altered. The assigned output width for E format must be at least 6 columns, and the assigned width minus the number of assigned decimal positions must be equal to or greater than 6.

D.6 COMMAw.d (Commas in Numbers)

As an input format with fixed data, COMMA is identical to F format, except that it can read numeric values with or without imbedded commas. For example, assuming keyword FIXED on DATA LIST, the values 1,234, 12,34 and 123,4 are all interpreted as 1234. In other words, the commas in the input values are ignored.

As an input format with freefield data, COMMA is identical to F format; thus, commas *cannot* be coded in the data (a comma in freefield data is interpreted as a delimiter).

The default output formats are COMMA, whether or not the input values have imbedded commas, and whether data are fixed or freefield. Thus, assuming there are no implied decimal positions in the input format, the input value 1234 is displayed in output as 1,234.

D.7 DOTw.d (Dots in Numbers)

The DOT format is similar to COMMA format, except the roles of the comma and the dot (period) are reversed. This is useful for reading and displaying numbers according to European conventions.

For input, DOT should be used only with fixed format data.

The default output formats are DOT. Thus, assuming there are no implied decimal positions in the input format, the input value 1234 is displayed as 1.234.

D.8 DOLLARw.d (Dollar Sign and Commas in Numbers)

As an input format with fixed data, DOLLAR is identical to F format, except that it can read numeric values with or without dollar signs and commas. For example, assuming keyword FIXED on DATA LIST, the values $1,234, 12,34 and 123,4 are all interpreted as 1234. In other words, dollar signs and commas in the input values are ignored. Only one leading dollar sign with no imbedded blanks can be coded into each value.

As an input format with freefield data, DOLLAR is identical to F format; thus, dollar signs and commas *cannot* be coded in the data (commas in freefield data are interpreted as delimiters).

The default output formats are DOLLAR, whether or not the input values have imbedded dollar signs and commas, and whether data are fixed or freefield. Thus, assuming there are no implied decimal positions in the input format, the input value 1234 is displayed in output as $1,234. (See the SET command for customizing currency formats for output.)

D.9 PCTw.d (Percent Sign after Numbers)

As an input format with fixed data, PCT is identical to F format, except that it can read numeric fields with or without a trailing percent sign. For example, assuming keyword FIXED on DATA LIST, the values 12 and 12% are both interpreted as 12. In other words, percent signs in the input values are ignored. Only one trailing percent sign with no imbedded blanks can be coded into each value.

As an input format with freefield data, PCT is identical to F format; thus, percent signs *cannot* be coded in the data.

The default output formats are PCT, whether or not the input values have imbedded percent signs, and whether data are fixed or freefield. Thus, assuming there are no implied decimal positions in the input format, the input value 12 is displayed in output as 12%.

The PCT format *does not* compute percentages, it just adds the percent sign to the value. The result of 1 divided by 2, for example, is displayed as .5% if PCT format is specified.

D.10 PIBHEXw (Hexadecimal of PIB)

The PIBHEX format interprets a series of hexadecimal characters as an unsigned integer. That is, FO is interpreted as 250 and FFFF is interpreted as 65,535. The values must be positive, and the width must be an even number. The maximum width specification is 16 columns. You cannot specify implied decimal digits.

The default output formats are an equivalent F format.

D.11 RBHEXw (Hexadecimal of RB)

The RBHEX format interprets a series of hexadecimal characters as a number that represents a floating-point number. This representation is highly implementation dependent. If the field width is less than twice the width of a floating-point number, padding with binary zeros occurs on the right. The values are real numbers, and the width must be an even number. (The exponent part is on the left on Intel 386 machines, which internally keep it on the right.)

The default output formats are an equivalent F format.

D.12 Zw.d (Zoned Decimal)

The z format reads data values that contain zoned decimal data. Such numbers may be generated by COBOL systems using DISPLAY data items, by PL/I systems using PICTURE data items, or by ASSEMBLER systems using zoned decimal data items.

In zoned decimal formats, ordinary decimal digits are used for all the digits except the last. The last digit carries sign information as well as a digit. The regular digits 0-9 are treated as positive. The left brace ({) is a zero digit with a positive sign; the letters A-I (upper case only) are the digits 1-9 with a positive sign. The right brace (}) is a zero digit with a negative sign, and the letters J-R are the digits 1-9 with a negative sign. Leading blanks and coded decimal points are allowed.

Sign   Digit

```
+      123456789
+      {ABCDEFGHI
−      }JKLMNOPQR
```

Zoned decimal is simply a formatted field in which the sign is an overpunch in the rightmost position.

The default output format is an equivalent F format.

D.13 Nonprintable Numeric Input Formats

Nonprintable numeric input formats apply to data that are readable only by machines. Generally, these formats adhere to the following conventions:

- Input blanks are treated as values and are not assigned system-missing.
- Each input format is converted to an equivalent F format for output.

D.14 IBw.d (Integer Binary)

The IB format reads fields that contain fixed-point binary (integer) data. The data might be generated by COBOL using COMPUTATIONAL data items, by FORTRAN using INTEGER*2 or INTEGER*4, or by ASSEMBLER systems using fullword and halfword items. The general format of binary items is a binary number of 16 or 32 bits in length using twos-complement notation for negative quantities.

For the IB format, w is the field width in bytes (omitted for column-style specifications) and d is the number of decimal digits to the right of the decimal point. Widths of 2 and 4 represent standard halfword and fullword integers, respectively. Single byte fields are treated as signed. For example, hexadecimal FF is read as -1.

D.15 PIBw.d (Positive Integer Binary)

The PIB format is essentially the same as IB, except that negative numbers are not allowed. This restriction allows one additional bit of magnitude.

D.16 Pw.d (Packed Decimal)

The P format is used to read fields with packed decimal numbers. Such numbers are generated by COBOL systems using COMPUTATIONAL–3 data items, and by ASSEMBLER systems using packed decimal data items. The general format of a packed decimal field is two four-bit digits in each byte of the field except the last. The last byte contains a single digit in its four leftmost bits and a four-bit sign in its rightmost bits. The number of digits in a field is $(2*w-1)$ where w is the field width in bytes. The sign is X'F' for positive values and X'D' for negative values (C zone equals F and E zone equals D). Remember, when defining a variable under P format, w is the number of bytes (not digits) and d is the number of digits to the right of the implied decimal point.

D.17 PKw.d (Unsigned Packed Decimal)

The PK format is essentially the same as P, except that there is no sign. That is, even the rightmost byte contains two digits, and negative data cannot be represented. One byte under PK format can represent numbers from 0 to 99, while under PIB one byte can represent numbers from 0 through 255.

D.18 RBw (Real Binary)

The RB format is used to read data values which contain internal format floating-point numbers. Such numbers are generated by COBOL systems using COMPUTATIONAL-1 or COMPUTATIONAL-2 data items, by PL/I systems using FLOATING DECIMAL data items, by FORTRAN systems using REAL or REAL*8 data items, or by ASSEMBLER systems using floating-point data items.

Normally, a width specification of 8 is used to read double-precision values, and a width of 4 is used to read single-precision values. The width specification must be an even number between 2 and 8.

D.19 String Formats

The string input formats are used to read character data. The values are either alphanumeric characters or the hexadecimal representation of alphanumeric characters. String formats conform to the following rules:

- Blank fields are interpreted as valid, not assigned system-missing.
- The default print and write formats are type A.

D.20 Aw (Standard Characters)

The A format is used to read standard characters. Characters can include letters, numbers, punctuation marks, blanks, and most other characters on your keyboard. This format defines a variable as a *string* variable; numbers entered as values for string variables cannot be used in calculations.

D.21 AHEXw (Hexadecimal Characters)

The AHEX format is used to read the hexadecimal representation of standard characters. On input, each set of two characters represents one standard character. The *w* specification must be an even number. By default, the output formats are of type A.

D.22 Date and Time Input Formats

Date and time formats are used to read values representing dates and times or date-time combinations. These formats translate values to "special" internal representations. The internal representation is up to 20 characters indicating the number of seconds from a fixed date (October 14, 1582), the number of seconds in a time interval, or an ordinal number.

- Date and time formats cannot be used with freefield input.
- There are eleven defined format codes. Each produces either a date, a time interval, or an ordinal number.

D.23 DATE

This format reads international dates in the form dd/mmm/yyyy. The following conventions apply:

- Two-digit years are assumed to be prefixed by 19.
- Months may be represented in digits, Roman numerals, three-character abbreviations, or fully spelled out: 10, X, OCT, OCTOBER, or October.
- Dashes, periods, commas, slashes, or blanks can be used as delimiters. For example, the date "December 2, 1984" can be expressed as 02-December-1984; 02.December.84; 02,December,1984; 02/December/1984; or 02 December 1984.
- The width defined on the DATA LIST command must be at least nine characters; however, data values of fewer characters are correctly evaluated.

D.24 ADATEw (American Date)

The ADATE format reads American format dates of the general form mm/dd/yyyy. As with DATE format, years may be represented as either two or four digits. Acceptable delimiters are blanks, dashes, periods, commas, or slashes. Months may be fully spelled out or represented as digits, Roman numerals, or three-character abbreviations. The width defined on the DATA LIST command must be at least eight characters. However, data values that have fewer characters are correctly evaluated.

D.25 JDATEw (Julian Date)

The JDATE format reads Julian-formatted dates in the form yyddd. If the number of digits read is five, a two-digit year is assumed, and 1900 will be added. A four-digit year is assumed if the number of digits is seven. The days field can be any number between 001 and 366. Leading zeros are required in the day field. No delimiters are allowed between the year and day fields. For example, the Julian equivalent of September 6, 1954, can be expressed as 1954249 but not as 1954/249.

D.26 QYRw (Quarter and Year)

The QYR format reads fields containing the quarter and the year in the form qQyyyy. The quarter is expressed as 1, 2, 3, or 4, and the year is represented by two or four digits. If two digits are used, 1900 is added. The quarter and year are separated by the letter Q. Blanks may be used as additional delimiters. The month is 3*(quarter−1)+1, and the day is 1. For example, April 1, 1958 is in the second quarter of 1958 and can be represented either as 2 Q 1958 or as 2Q1958.

D.27 MOYRw (Month and Year)

The MOYR format reads values in the form mm/yyyy. Months can be expressed as digits, Roman numerals, three-character abbreviations (as in JAN, FEB, and so on), or they may be spelled out. The year is expressed as either two or four digits. If it is two digits, 1900 is added. Blanks, dashes, periods, commas, or slashes can be used as delimiters. The "days" portion of the date is assumed to be 1. The width defined on the DATA LIST command must be at least six characters; however, data values of fewer characters are correctly evaluated.

D.28 WKYRw (Week and Year)

The WKYR format reads dates in the form wkWKyyyy. A week is expressed as a number from 1 to 53. The year is a two- or four-digit number. Week 1 is assumed to begin on 1 JAN, week 2 on 8 JAN, and so forth. The week and year are separated by the string WK. Blanks can be used as additional delimiters. For example, you can express the 14th week of 1984 as either 14 WK 1984 or as 14WK1984. The width defined on the DATA LIST command must be at least six characters; however, data values of five characters are correctly evaluated.

D.29 TIMEw (Time)

The TIME format is used to read a time of day or a time interval into a datum of type time interval. The input field is of the form hh:mm:ss.ss. The following conventions apply:

- Colons, blanks, or periods may be used as delimiters between hours, minutes, and seconds. A period is required to separate seconds from fractional seconds.
- Input fields must contain hours and minutes. Seconds and fractional seconds may be omitted and will default to zeros. Thus, the field 23:59 when read under TIME format will result in 23:59:00.

- Data values can contain a sign.
- Fractional seconds must have the decimal point coded in the data value.
- Hours may be of unlimited magnitude. The maximum for minutes is 59; for seconds, 59.99....

D.30 DTIMEw (Days and Time)

The DTIME format is used to read a time interval that includes days in the form ddd hh:mm:ss.ss, such as 12 23:44:01.58 or 144 18:40. The number of days is separated from the hours by an acceptable TIME delimiter: a blank, a period, or a colon. A preceding sign $(+/-)$ may be used. The remainder of the field must conform to required specifications for the TIME format. Fractional seconds must have the decimal point coded in the data value.

D.31 DATETIMEw (Date and Time)

The DATETIME format is used to read values containing a date and a time. The date must be written as an international date (dd-mmm-yyyy) followed by a blank and then a time in the form hh:mm:ss.ss, such as 14-OCT-1977 14:12:51.10. The time conforms to a twenty-four-hour clock. Thus the maximum subfields for time are 23 for hours, 59 for minutes, and 59.999... for seconds.

Fractional seconds must have the decimal point coded in the data value. The width defined on the DATA LIST command must be at least 17 characters; however, data values of fewer characters are correctly evaluated.

D.32 WKDAYw (Day of the Week)

The WKDAY format is used to read the day of the week expressed as a character string. Only the first two characters are significant, and the minimum field width is two. Remaining characters are optional: Sunday could be expressed as SUNDAY or as SU. Though the input values must be entered as strings, SPSS translates them to integers between 1 and 7, where Sunday equals 1 and Saturday equals 7. Thus, the values are numeric and cannot be treated as strings. For example, you cannot use the string function CONCAT to concatenate WKDAY with MONTH. The output values are displayed as strings. To display the values as integers, use FORMATS to define F formats for the output.

D.33 MONTHw (Month)

The MONTH format is used to read the month of the year expressed as a character string. Names may be fully spelled out, for example OCTOBER, or abbreviated to three characters. For example, OCTOBER could be written as OCT. In addition, input values can be entered as integers between 1 and 12, where January equals 1 and December equals 12. Whether the values are entered as strings or integers, SPSS translates them to integers between 1 and 12. Thus, the values are numeric and cannot be treated as strings. For example, you cannot use the string function CONCAT to concatenate WKDAY with MONTH. The output values are displayed as strings. To display the values as integers, use FORMATS to define F formats for the output.

D.34 T AND X FORMAT ELEMENTS

The T and X format elements skip columns you do not want to define. The T and X elements are available only as input formats for fixed data. If T and X elements are specified with freefield data, the element specifications are ignored.

- The element *Tn* tabs to the column number specified by *n*. The next format element defines the variable to be read beginning in that column.
- The T format element can be used to move backward and forward within the same record.
- The element *n*X skips *n* columns. The next format element defines the variable to be read beginning with the column *following* the skip.
- If two or more variables are recorded in adjacent columns of the same record and have the same format type, width, and number of implied decimal places, they can be defined by specifying the number of adjacent variables before the format element.
- Several format elements can be combined into a *format list* within the same set of parentheses to define a list of variables. The variable list can include individual variable names and variable names defined using keyword TO. The format element or format list enclosed in parentheses follows the variable name or variable list to which it applies.

Example.

```
DATA LIST  FILE=HUBDATA RECORDS=3
 / MOHIRED (T12,F2.0).
```

- Variable MOHIRED is located in columns 12 and 13.

Example.

```
DATA LIST  FILE=HUBDATA RECORDS=3
 /MOHIRED (11X,F2.0).
```

- The x element is used to make the same specification made by the T element in the previous example.

Example.

```
DATA LIST  FILE=HUBDATA RECORDS=3
 /1 ID (T19,F3.0) LNAME (T12,A20)
 /2 MOHIRED, YRHIRED, DEPT1 TO DEPT4 (T12,2F2.0,4F1.0).
```

- The first defined variable on record 1 is ID, located in column 19. Variable ID is a numeric variable with a width of 3 characters. The second variable on record 1 is LNAME, located in columns 12 through 31. Variable LNAME is a string variable with a width of 20 characters.
- The next set of defined variables is located on record 2. The T12 format element in the format list positions the next data format element in column 12.
- The first variable, MOHIRED, is a two-column integer variable located in columns 12 and 13. The second variable, YRHIRED, also a two-column integer variable, is located in columns 14 and 15. The next four variables, DEPT1 through DEPT4, are single-column variables located in columns 16 through 19.

D.35 COLUMN BINARY FORMAT

Column binary formats are used to define data stored on computer cards, tapes, or disks that use the *column binary* (also called *multipunch*) method of storing data. The general format for each variable with a column binary format is

```
varname starting column:starting row - ending column:ending row
```

SPSS only processes multipunch data that have been read by IBM card readers attached to IBM 360-compatible computers. These readers produce a particular representation of the punches.

- The FILE HANDLE command is required for reading column binary data. The file handle must match the handle named on the FILE subcommand on DATA LIST. In addition, MODE=MULTIPUNCH must be specified on FILE HANDLE to specify the file as column binary. Variables can then be defined on DATA LIST.

- Once a file has been specified as column binary, variables must then be defined on the DATA LIST command (or a REPEATING DATA, or REREAD command). Starting and ending rows as well as columns must be specified for each variable. The starting column and row are required and must be separated by a colon. The ending row and column are optional if they are the same as the starting row and column.

- No more than one punch is allowed in any given field. Any attempt to read fields that contain more than one punch will produce an error, resulting in the system-missing value for the variable. In situations where more than one response is permitted to a question, each response must be coded as a separate variable.

- Although multipunch columns can be read only by using column binary format, all other formats can be used to read single-punched columns in the same data file.

- Frequently, data stored in column binary format use the 11 punch and the 12 punch (in EBCDIC these are minus signs and ampersands) to represent responses like "don't know," "no answer," or "nonapplicable." When using a non-column binary format, variables containing these values must be read in as string variables. Use the keyword CONVERT on the RECODE command to transform the alphanumeric values '&' and '−' to the numeric values 11 and 12, as in

```
RECODE V1 ('-'=11) ('&'=12) (CONVERT) INTO V2.
```

D.36 Limitations

- Multipunched files can only be referenced on three commands: DATA LIST, REPEATING DATA, and REREAD. Cases cannot be defined with FILE TYPE. For example, you cannot specify FILE TYPE MIXED.

Example.

```
FILE HANDLE  ELE48  MODE=MULTIPUNCH
  /NAME='E:\DATA\ELECTION.RES'.
DATA LIST FILE=ELE48
    /1 PARTY     18
       SEX       19:1
       EMPSTAT   20(A)
       SES       48:4-6
       RELIGION  48:7-10
       OCCUPAT   50:11-51:2.
RECODE EMPSTAT (CONVERT) ('-'=11)('&'=12) INTO EMPSTAT2.
```

- The FILE HANDLE command defines handle ELE48 for the data. MODE = MULTIPUNCH identifies data as column binary data. The NAME subcommand locates the data on device E: in the directory E:\DATA. The file is identified as ELECTION.RES.
- The DATA LIST command defines variables for the file referenced by the handle ELE48. Variable SEX is located in row 1 of column 19, SES in rows 4 through 6 of column 48, RELIGION in rows 7 through 10 of column 48, and OCCUPAT in column 50:row 11 through column 51:row 2. Since columns 18 and 20 were not multipunched, the column numbers alone are sufficient to define the location of PARTY and EMPSTAT.
- A standard numeric format is used to read the variable PARTY.
- All numbers in string variable EMPSTAT are recoded to numbers for target variable EMPSTAT2. In addition, the minus sign is changed to 11 and the ampersand to 12.

D.37 Column Binary Data on Disk

Column binary data occur in fixed-length records containing an even number of bytes, normally 160. Each column of the original input card is recorded in two adjacent bytes of a record. Thus, the second column of the original input card is recorded in the third and fourth bytes of the record. The top six rows of the first column of the original card are represented by the rightmost six bits of the first byte, and the bottom six rows of the first column are represented by the rightmost six bits of the second byte. The first two bits (leftmost) of each byte are always set to zero (see Table D.37a). For example, a 2 punch (bit 7 of the first byte) is represented as B'00000010', and a 5 punch (bit 4 of the second byte) is represented as B'00010000'.

Table D.37a *Bit, row, and punch correspondences*

	First byte						Second byte					
Bit	3	4	5	6	7	8	3	4	5	6	7	8
Row	1	2	3	4	5	6	7	8	9	10	11	12
Punch	12	11	0	1	2	3	4	5	6	7	8	9

D.38 UNALIGNED POSITIVE INTEGER BINARY FORMAT

Unaligned positive integer binary format (known as UPIB format) permits you to read positive integer binary (PIB) fields that do not begin and end on byte boundaries. This feature allows you to read individual bits within fields or to read fields that contain a combination of punches as one variable.

- Fields are defined according to starting and ending byte and bit locations.
- If multiple adjacent fields containing equal numbers of bits are to be read, the location information follows the list of variable names.

Note: UPIB formats that span byte boundaries should not be used.

D.39 UPIB versus Column Binary Format

The UPIB format also reads multipunched data. Fields to be read under UPIB format are specified with a syntax identical to that used for column binary. In fact, when used to read single-bit dichotomies, the two formats produce results that are identical. The determination of which type of field the user specified is made by examining the declared data mode of the input field. If the data mode was declared to be MULTIPUNCHED on the FILE HANDLE command, the field is assumed to be column binary. If the data mode was not specifically declared to be multipunched, the field is assumed to be unaligned binary. There are three additional differences between column binary and unaligned positive integer binary:

- The column binary format specifies which rows are to be read from virtual card columns. The UPIB format specifies which bits are to be read from actual bytes.
- The column binary format is restricted to records containing a maximum of 80 virtual card columns. The UPIB format can be used when reading a record of any length supported by SPSS.
- For each field, the column binary format expects at most a single punch on a given case and returns the ordinal position of the punch that occurs. The UPIB format accepts any combination of bits and returns the binary integer represented by the bits that are on.

D.40 Limitations

- Unaligned binary input field specifications are valid only on DATA LIST, KEYED DATA LIST, and REPEATING DATA.

- The maximum number of bits that can be specified for any single variable is 64. On machines that support OS, DOS, and CMS operating systems, a maximum of 56 significant bits will be retained when reading fields over 56 bits in width.
- Fields to be read as unaligned binary integers are always treated as positive. No parenthesized format type is permitted following the location information. The variables defined are assigned print and write formats of F.

Example.

```
DATA LIST FILE=FILEIN
   / USERTYPE 1:1-2
     CPUTIME  1:3-4:7
   V1 TO V5 10:3-7.
```

- Variable USERTYPE is in bits 1 and 2 of byte 1; CPUTIME is defined as a series of bits that begins in bit 3 of byte 1 and ends in bit 7 of byte 4.
- For variables V1 to V5, five single-bit variables will be read from bits 3 through 7 of column 10 of the input record. The contents of each field are read as the positive integer represented in binary by the combination of bits within the field.

Example.

```
DATA LIST  FILE=PSWS
   /PERMASK 1:2             /*Program Event Recording Mask
    TRANSMODE               /*Translation Mode
    IOMASK                  /*Input/Output Mask
    EXTMASK 1:6-8           /*External Mask
    PROTKEY 2:1-4           /*Protection Key
    ECMODE                  /*EC Mode=1
    MCMASK                  /*Machine Check Mask
    WAIT                    /*Wait State
    PROB    2:5-8           /*Problem State
    CC      3:3-4           /*Condition Code
    FXOVMASK                /*Fixed Point Overflow Mask
    DCOVMASK                /*Decimal Overflow Mask
    EXUFMASK                /*Exponent Underflow Mask
    SIGMASK 3:5-8
    ADDRESS 5-8 (PIB).   /*Instruction Address
```

- This example illustrates interpreting the IBM machine Program Status Word (EC mode). The protection key is four bits long, the condition code is two bits, and the instruction address is three bytes long. All the other fields are single bits.

Index

A (format), 143
About SPSS
  menu command, 45
ADATE (format), 144
add blank line, 98-99
ADEVICE (subcommand)
  SET command, 105
AHEX (format), 143
analysis
  perform, 30-31
analyze data (menu option), 23-28
Append Selection
  menu command, 48
append text
  to end of file, 99
Append Window
  menu command, 48
Apple menu, 45
applications
  with SPSS, 117
Arrange All
  menu command, 62

begin an SPSS session
  reference, 70-72
  tutorial, 19-21
BEGIN DATA (command)
  pasting, 75
binary data, 142
BOX (subcommand)
  SET command, 104
button, 94
  activating, 117
  Glossary window, 64
  Next, 73
  on Help window, 89

CASEFILE subcommand
  CRICKET command, 131-132
Characters
  type, 101
Clear
  menu command, 55
Close
  menu command, 47
close box, 114-115
column binary files, 84
column binary format, 148-150

COMMA (format), 139
command
  add to a file, 39-40
  enter, 19-34, 73-76
  EXPORT, 86
  GET TRANSLATE, 82-83
  IMPORT, 82
  insert from a file, 41-42
  interrupt running, 78
  load from a file, 76-77
  menu bar or SPSS, 15
  paste, 73-74
  refer to file, 87-88
  rules, 73
  run, 31, 37-38, 77, 117
  SAVE, 86
  SAVE TRANSLATE, 86-87
  select, 53, 56
  select from an SPSS menu, 73-74
  SPSS, how to use, 72-78
  type into window, 76
  XSAVE, 86
command file, 78-79
  create, 78
  in word processor, 78
  open, 35-37, 79
  save, 40-41, 79
  summary of use, 43
  use, 35-43
  Value.Commands, 35-37
  ValueDescr.Commands, 43
  ValueFormat.Commands, 41
  ValueFreq.Commands, 43
  ValueMeans.Commands, 43
  ValuePlot.Commands, 43
  ValueReport.Commands, 41-42
Command Generator window, 62
  use, 23-26
command, SPSS
  exceptions, 104-106
commands
  added to SPSS for the Macintosh, 14
  not available, 14
Copy
  menu command, 54, 99
Copy Table
  menu command, 55
COUNT (function)
  CRICKET command, 131

CRICKET (command), 118-132
   aggregation functions, 130-131
   CASEFILE subcommand, 131-132
   count functions, 131
   examples, 129
   functions, 130-131
   limitations, 129
   reference, 126-132
   summary functions, 130-131
   syntax, 126-127
   TABLE subcommand, 129-131
Cricket Graph
   copy table from SPSS, 55
   draw graph, 119-120
CUFREQ (function)
   CRICKET command, 131
CUPCT (function)
   CRICKET command, 131
customizing a session, 71-72
CUSUM (function)
   CRICKET command, 130
Cut
   menu command, 54, 100

data file
   get, 21-23
data files, 80-88
   column binary, 84
   creation, 8
   fixed record-length files, 84
   multipunch files, 84
   reading raw, 83
   types, 8-9
DATE (format), 144
date and time input formats, 143-147
DATETIME (format), 146
decimal positions
   implied, 134
Delete
   menu command, 100
delete key, 14
DESCRIPTIVES (command)
   in command file, 43
   practice, 32
deselect text, 103
directory
   setting for SPSS commands, 95-96
DIRECTORY (subcommand)
   SET command, 105
directory dialog box, 92-95
document
   file or SPSS command, 15
DOT (format), 139-140
DRAW (subcommand)
   SET command, 105
Drawing Graphs, 118-132
DTIME (format), 146

E (format), 138-139
Edit
   text in SPSS, 97-103
Edit menu, 52-58, 98-100
end an SPSS session, 33
end and SPSS session, 91
ENDCMD (subcommand)
   SET command, 105
enter commands, 23-26, 73-76
Enter key
   running commands, 117
ERRORS (subcommand)
   SET command, 104
example
   CRICKET command, 120-132
Excel
   copy table from SPSS, 55
Excel file, 80
EXPORT command, 86

F (format), 137-138
fieldnames
   saving, 87
FIELDNAMES (subcommand)
   GET TRANSLATE command, 82
file
   add command, 39-40
   create, 78
   data, 80-88
   database, 80
   Excel, 80
   get data, 80-83
   Multiplan, 80-82
   naming, 85
   on SPSS command, 87-88
   open, 79, 94
   open data, 80-83
   raw data, 80-83
   removing SPSS module, 113
   save, 91-96
   save commands, 79
   save data, 85
   save SPSS system, 85
   select, 91-96
   select from dialog box, 36
   spreadsheet, 80
   SPSS portable, 80
   SPSS system, 80-81
   tab-delimited, 80
   temporary, 72
   type, 92
   update SPSS modules, 113
FILE HANDLE (command), 84
   long pathname, 88
File menu, 35-36, 45-52
   Append option, 99
files
   number open, 108

Find
  menu command, 58-60
formats, 133-152
  column binary data, 148-150
  input, 133-152
  multipunch data, 148-152
  nonprintable numeric formats,
      141-143
  output, 133-152
  printable numeric formats, 137-141
  string numeric formats, 143
  T and X format elements, 147-148
  time and date formats, 143-147
  unaligned positive integer binary data,
      151-152
FORMATS (command), 39-40
FREQ (function)
  CRICKET command, 131
FREQUENCIES (command), 30-32
  in command file, 43
functions
  CRICKET command, 130-131

GCMDFILE (subcommand)
  SET command, 105
GDATA (subcommand)
  SET command, 105
GDEVICE (subcommand)
  SET command, 105
GET (command), 81
Get Data File, 80-83
  menu command, 49
Get SPSS System File
  menu command, 48
Get SPSS System File (menu
      command), 81
GET TRANSLATE
  SPSS command, 105-106
GET TRANSLATE (command), 81-83
Glossary window, 62-64
  paste definitions, 100-101
GMEMORY (subcommand)
  SET command, 105
graph, 118-132
  change scale, 122
  examples, 120-132
  histogram, 126
  line, 121-122
  pie, 123
  scatterplot, 123-125
graph settings, 105

Help
  button, 89
  online, 9, 89-90
  SPSS, 89
  syntax diagrams, 89-90

Help menu, 68-69
histogram, 126

IB (format), 142
IMAGE (keyword)
  FILE HANDLE command, 84
implied decimal positions, 134
IMPORT (command), 81-82
INFO (command), 106
input data formats
  table, 135
Input window, 20, 68
  contents, 36-38
  enter and run commands, 72-78
  menu command, 68
  new, 78
Insertion point
  description, 97
  move with arrow keys, 97-98
  move with mouse, 97
install SPSS for the Macintosh, 107-113
  machine requirements, 107
  modules, 111-112
  remove optional modules, 113
  start Setup, 111
  update program modules, 113
installing modules, 111-112
interrupt processing, 78

JDATE (format), 144
join lines, 100
JOURNAL (subcommand)
  SET command, 105

keys
  mouse keys, 115

line graph, 121-122
lines
  join, 100
  select, 56
  split, 101
LIST (command)
  example, 23-28
listing file, 90-91
load commands from a file, 76-77
LRECL (subcommand)
  FILE HANDLE command, 84

Macintosh
  concepts, 114-117
manual organization, 4
manuals available, 2-3
MAXIMUM (function)
  CRICKET command, 130
MEAN (function)
  CRICKET command, 130

MEANS (command)
  in command file, 43
  practice, 32
MEDIAN (function)
  CRICKET command, 131
memory required, 107
menu, 44-69
  Apple, 45
  Edit, 52-58
  File, 45-52
  Help, 68-69
  Run, 60-61
  Search, 58-60
  shortcut, 74
  Window, 61-68
menu selections
  Command Generator window, 73-74
menus
  two types, 6-7
menus, SPSS
  explore, 74-75
  navigating, 74
  paste selections, 75-76
MESSAGES (subcommand)
  SET command, 104
Microsoft Word
  copy table from SPSS, 55
MINIMUM (function)
  CRICKET command, 130
MODE (function)
  CRICKET command, 131
MODE (subcommand)
  FILE HANDLE command, 84
module
  installing, 111-112
  removing, 111-113
MONTH (format), 147
mouse
  move insertion point, 97
move text, 100
MOYR (format), 145
Multiplan file, 80
multiple applications, 117
MULTIPUNCH (keyword)
  FILE HANDLE command, 84
multipunch format, 148-152
MXERRS (subcommand)
  SET command, 105
MXWARNS (subcommand)
  SET command, 105

N (format), 138
N (function)
  CRICKET command, 130
NAME (subcommand)
  FILE HANDLE command, 84
New (menu command), 46
  command file, 78

Next button, 73, 74-75
NGT (function)
  CRICKET command, 131
NIN (function)
  CRICKET command, 131
NLT (function)
  CRICKET command, 131
nonprintable numeric formats, 141-143
numbers
  round off, 101
  truncate, 101

online documentation, 3
online help, 89-90
online syntax diagrams, 89-90
Open
  menu command, 46-47
Open (menu command), 79
output
  view, 32, 78
output data formats
  table, 136
Output window, 20, 67
  contents, 38-40
  menu command, 67
  scrolling, 78
  select lines, 56
overview, 5-18

P (format), 142
Page Setup
  menu command, 50
paste
  BEGIN DATA command, 75
  commands, 24-26, 73-74
  from glossary window, 100-101
  glossary definitions, 64
  menu command, 54-55
  menu selections, 75-76
  variable name, 67
pathname
  how to specify, 88
  instead of SET DIRECTORY, 87
  long, 88
PCT (format), 140
PCT (function)
  CRICKET command, 131
period missing, 77
PGT (function)
  CRICKET command, 131
PIB (format), 142
PIBHEX (format), 140
pie chart, 123
PIN (function)
  CRICKET command, 131
PK (format), 142

PLOT (command)
  in command file, 43
  practice, 32
PLT (function)
  CRICKET command, 131
pointer
  moving with keys, 115
practice suggestions, 32
  command files, 42-43
Preferences
  menu command, 56-58
Preferences (menu command), 71-72
Prev. button, 74
Print Selection
  menu command, 51
Print Window
  menu command, 50-51
printable numeric formats, 137-141
PRINTBACK (subcommand)
  SET command, 104
printing, 116-117
PTILE (function)
  CRICKET command, 131

Quit
  menu command, 52
QUIT (menu command), 91
QYR (format), 145

range
  spreadsheet, 83
RANGE (subcommand)
  GET TRANSLATE command, 83
raw data file, 80-83
  reading, 83
RB (format), 143
RBHEX (format), 140-141
Read Me file, 106, 108
rearrange windows, 71
Redo
  menu command, 54
removing modules, 111-113
replace text, 60
requirements for installation, 107
RESULTS (subcommand)
  SET command, 104
Return key and Enter key, 117
Round
  menu command, 55-56
round numbers, 101
run
  commands, 26-28, 77
  commands in a file, 37-38
  CRICKET command, 118-119
run commands, 117
Run menu, 60-61

Run Selection
  menu command, 60-61
run SPSS, 70-96

save
  command file, 40-41, 79
  data file, 85-86
  menu command, 47-48
  SPSS system file, 85
SAVE (command), 86
  pasting, 85
Save (menu command)
  command file, 79
Save As (menu command), 48
  command file, 79
Save Data File (menu command), 50, 86
Save SPSS System File
  menu command, 48
SAVE TRANSLATE (command), 86-87
scale
  graph, 122
scatterplot, 123-125
scroll window
  with mouse, 115-116
Search and Replace
  menu command, 60
Search entry (text box), 63
Search menu, 58-60
select commands, 56
select commands from a menu, 73-74
select text, 53, 101-103
SET (command)
  additional subcommands, 105
  subcommand exceptions, 104
  subcommands not available, 105
SET command
  page size, 116-117
Set Directory
  menu command, 51-52, 95-96
SET DIRECTORY (command), 87-88
Set Directory (menu option), 87-88
Setup (program)
  install optional modules, 111-112
  install SPSS for the Macintosh,
    107-113
  remove optional modules, 113
  Setup window, 109-110
  start Setup, 111
  update program modules, 113
shortcut to menu selections, 74
size box, 114-115
special variables, 66
split lines, 101
spreadsheet
  ranges, 83

SPSS
   features, 6-9
   typical session, 9-13
   with other applications, 117
SPSS command
   exceptions, 104-106
   how to use, 72-78
   paste, 24-26
   running, 26-28
SPSS command file, see command file
SPSS for Macintosh
   run, 70-96
SPSS for the Macintosh
   compared with SPSS/PC+, 15-18
   user needs to know, 5
SPSS portable file, 80
SPSS session
   begin, 19-21, 70-72
   end, 33
   initial windows, 20-21
   run SPSS, 70-96
   summary, 34
SPSS system file, 80
SPSS/PC+
   compared with SPSS for the
     Macintosh, 15-18
SPSSfont
   install, 112
status dialog box, 20-21
STDDEV (function)
   CRICKET command, 130
string formats, 143
SUM (function)
   CRICKET command, 130
summary function
   CRICKET command, 130-131
SYLK
   file type, 92
syntax diagrams
   online, 89-90
SYS
   file type, 92
system disks
   preparing, 110
system file
   SPSS or Macintosh, 15
system variables, 66

T and X format elements, 147-148
tab-delimited file, 80
tab-delimited files
   fieldnames, 87
TABLE subcommand
   CRICKET command, 129-131
TB2 (subcommand)
   SET command, 105
temporary file
   storage, 72

text
   deselect, 103
   file type, 92
   move, 100
   select, 53, 101-103
TIME (format), 145-146
time input formats, 143-147
truncate numbers, 101
tutorial
   CRICKET graphs, 118-120
   enter SPSS commands, 19-34
   use SPSS command file, 35-43
TYPE (subcommand)
   GET TRANSLATE command, 82
   SAVE TRANSLATE command, 86-87
type a command, 76
types of files, 92
typing specifications, 26

**unaligned positive integer binary format,
   151-152**
Undo
   menu command, 54
untitled document, 46
update SPSS for the Macintosh program
   files, 113

**ValueDescr.Commands (command file),
   43**
ValueFormat.Commands file, 41
ValueFreq.Commands (command file),
   43
value labels, 64
ValueMeans.Commands (command file),
   43
ValuePlot.Commands (command file),
   43
ValueReport.Commands file, 41-42
variable
   CRICKET label, 128
   labels, 66
   names, 66
   paste name, 67
variable names, 9
variables
   keep, drop, rename, 85
Variables window
   menu command, 64-67
   paste variable names, 31
   use, 28-29
VARIANCE (function)
   CRICKET command, 131
vector names, 66

width of windows, 72
Window menu, 61-68
   select Command Generator, 23

windows, 44-68
    Command Generator, 62
    Glossary, 62-64
    Input, 68
    jump or not, 71
    manipulating, 114-115
    Output, 67
    scroll, 115-116
    Variables, 64-67
    view more lines, 36
WKDAY (format), 146
WKYR (format), 145
workspace, 71

XSAVE (command), 86
XSORT (subcommand)
    SET command, 105

Z (format), 141
zoom box, 114-115